Redefining

Red and Green

To Randy --
thank you for
your support
of 2 starving
grad students

SUNY series in
International Environmental Policy and Theory

Sheldon Kamieniecki, editor

$\mathcal{R}$edefining

Red and Green

Ideology and Strategy in
European Political Ecology

Tad Shull

State University of New York Press

Published by
State University of New York Press, Albany

© 1999 State University of New York

All rights reserved

Printed in the United States of America

For information, address the State University of New York Press,
State University Plaza, Albany, NY 12246

Production by Laurie Searl
Marketing by Patrick Durocher

Library of Congress Cataloging-in-Publication Data

Shull, Tad.
    Redefining red and green : ideology and strategy in European
political ecology / Tad Shull.
        p.   cm. — (SUNY series in international environmental policy
and theory)
    Includes bibliographical references and index.
    ISBN 0–7914–4041–9 (hardcover   :   alk. paper). — ISBN
0–7914–4042–7   (pbk.   :   alk. paper)
    1. Grünen (Political party)   2. Green movement—Germany.
3. Environmental policy—Germany.   4. Verts (Political party)
5. Green movement—France.   6. Environmental policy—France.
I. Title.   II. Series.
JN3971.A98G723753   1999
    324.2′187′094—dc21   98–26815
                                                                                        CIP

10 9 8 7 6 5 4 3 2 1

While we fancy ourselves going straight forward, and attaining, at every step, an entirely new position of affairs, we do actually return to something long ago tried and abandoned, but which we now find etherialized, refined, and perfected to its ideal.

—Nathaniel Hawthorne, *The House of the Seven Gables*

Contents

Chapter Five

Chapter Six

Chapter Seven

Chapter Eight

Chapter Nine

Chapter Ten

$\mathcal{F}$oreword

As this book went to press, a Europe already dogged by uncertainty beheld one further change. The continent faced a transition to a single currency, the millennium bug, and a spreading crisis of emerging markets, not to mention unemployment and xenophobia. Then European citizens awoke on Monday, September 28 to find that the normally risk-averse Germans had begun an experiment the day before. No sitting chancellor had ever been voted out of office in postwar Germany. But voters had indeed ushered out Chancellor Helmut Kohl, the force behind unification and a pillar of Europe's construction. A relatively untested challenger, Gerhardt Schröder, would now steer one of the world's biggest economies. Schröder's party, the Social Democrats (SPD), received 40.9% of the vote. This was a far larger margin over the outgoing Christian Democrats (with 35.2%) than anyone had expected.

Schröder, a former militant leader of the SPD's youth wing, began traveling three days later to assure the heads of Western nations of Germany's reliability and stability under his stewardship. They were avid listeners. Like Schröder, Jospin, Blair, and Clinton were all "modernizers" of their left-of-center parties. All were honed by 'sixties activism but sobered by the prospect of holding real power. In choosing candidates of the "new center" over right-wing incumbents, voters seem to have been demanding that their governments strike a balance between the market and social rights. Despite immense political skills, none of these leaders has found this balance yet.

The most extraordinary thing about the new German government was that members of the Green Party (*Bundnis '90 / Die Grünen*) would join it. The latter won 6.7% and 47 seats. Both parties' voters had been aware that if Schröder won he would ask the Greens to help form the government. As it turned out, the red/green coalition would have a 21-seat majority in the *Bundestag*. This was clearly a mandate for change.

Germany will not be the only European country in which ecologists participate in the government; in that it joins France, Finland, Sweden, and Italy. But nowhere do the ecologists have the stature and potential influence they may have in the Federal Republic. It is customary in Germany that the junior coalition partner be appointed foreign minister. Joschka Fischer, the leader of the Greens' parliamentary faction, has been named to that post.

While Schröder assures the world of his country's stability, Fischer and his party must reassure Schröder of their fitness to govern. That, too, requires a delicate balance. Fischer is a pragmatist who plays to the mainstream voter and politician. His party has long treated him with suspicion and sometimes outright rebelliousness for that very reason. Many of these rank-and-file members oppose NATO and support drastic eco-taxes. On the SPD side, Schröder, who has a far stronger electorate mandate, is little inclined to grant policy concessions to the Greens.

The Greens and the SPD have always been both natural partners and fierce adversaries. Current talks on forming a Green/SPD governing coalition have found common ground on social policy. Schröder's promised "Alliance for Jobs" would speed unemployed young people's placement in training positions. A tax reform would stimulate demand by benefiting working families. Thornier territory lies ahead in foreign policy and energy. While Green leaders have relaxed both their demands to exit NATO and their opposition to sending German troops to Kosovo, the majority of the party has not. There are sharp disagreements on the timing of a phaseout from nuclear power and on the Greens' demand to triple gasoline taxes. Talks may stumble on another of the Greens' core principles: strict male-female parity in the party leadership. Although the Greens want four ministries, the SPD is set on granting only three. Jürgen Trittin, leader of the Greens' left wing, will join Fischer in the government as environmental minister. That leaves one sole post for a woman, and another principle sacrificed to the exigencies of power.

The challenge for the European greens will be to show they have a positive role to play in government without surrendering the democratic and ecological principles they have lived by. They have to propose viable solutions to environmental and social problems without alienating either their constituents or mainstream voters and politicians. They have to support their coalitions without being outflanked or marginalized by their center-left partners. When ecology candidates were first elected to local offices more than twenty years ago, they faced the same challenges. Today, the stakes are higher and the dilemmas more exquisite. The ideas that define the greens when they enter politics, and the practical choices they make when they arrive at the doors of power, are the concern of the pages that follow.

Tad Shull
October 1998

Preface

This book has its origins in a simple empirical observation. The French ecologists, like France in the Western Alliance, wanted to be different. The *Verts* were particularly concerned with their own autonomy and independence, and they were trying to discover a political discourse that set them apart from other parties, including other green parties. Fortified by the poor prospects for environmentalism in France, the *Verts* refined their ideas to a point where they had an unalloyed and lucid version of an ecological worldview, as much so as any that could be found. This had to be important. New and comprehensive ideas are after all the stock in trade of new parties with unfamiliar demands.

Asking why the *Verts* stood apart, it became clear that it was the French Left itself that was different during the 1980s. It was marching in a leftward direction while other socialists or social democrats were in decline or retreat. The *Verts* needed to amplify their pleas in order to be heard above the clamor of the Left's first heady days in power under the Fifth Republic. From there the larger questions emerged: why should progressive organizations concerned with emancipatory reform wind up competing with each other? What were the consequences of these political divisions? Whatever the differences, was there anything common to green and red? Was there some dynamic that governed all progressive parties, whatever their demands? These are the political and theoretical problems this book seeks to address.

Scholars interested in progressive politics need to take stock of the competition and fragmentation besetting the Left everywhere. Perhaps with the intuition that "truth is one," and that all good things go together, sympathetic observers of Green and Red have assumed that all would be right if their ideologies, and by extension, the organizations that bear them, should simply fuse. Thus we hear that the ecologists should be more "responsible," and cooperate with the mainstream parties, or that the red/green fusion would represent the best of both worlds. While the ecological and the social both are important, there is too much at stake in each one to expect an easy synthesis. The ecologists have a clear interest in ensuring the pace of reform, and the older parties of the Left in resisting it. It is true that the whole state of the debate may have been enriched by the competition between red and green. The task for now is to ask what strategy will keep up the pressure for reforms. At the same time, ecologists are still perceived as preaching more scarcity in a world of scarce resources, including scarce social and ethical resources. They need to confront the political consequences of that fact, and that the strongest pressure on their side may come from the established representatives of social emancipation.

I would like to thank the *Verts* collectively for their candor and their willingness to provide information about their party and its place in French politics. I would like to thank the following individual members for taking the time to share their thoughts with me: Marie-Christine Aulas, Christian Brodhag, Yves Cochet, Jean-Paul Deléage, Marie-Françoise Mendez, Gérard Monnier-Besombes, Pierre Radanne, and Jacky Walsh. Environmentalist Jean-Pierre Raffin also lent his valuable time, along with Pierre Orselly of the Socialist Party. I should also thank two particularly astute observers of the ecology movement and of French politics, Guillaume Sainteny and Daniel Boy, for sharing their insights.

Finally, I must thank my mentors and colleagues at Columbia University for their help and criticism. Since they were involved at so many different junctures, it seems as though the ideas contained here are theirs as much as mine. Special thanks, then, to Doug Barnes, Tim Christenfeld, Jean Cohen, David Gallagher, Peter Johnson, Mark Kesselman, Allan Silver, and Kent Worcester. Kerry Whiteside of Franklin and Marshall College and Joel Krieger of Wellesley College also gave insightful readings and valuable comments. Above all, I thank my wife, Sigrun Kaland, for everything.

Abbreviations

France

ADEME   Agence de l'Environnement et de la Maîtrise de l'Énergie (Agency for the Environment and Energy Autonomy)

AREV   Alternative Rouge et Vert (Red and Green Alternative)

CNIR   Conseil National Inter-Régionale (National Interregional Council, the Verts' Internal Parliament)

CE   Confédération Écologiste (Ecologist Confederation)

CES   Convergences Écologie Solidarité (Ecology Solidarity Convergences)

CFDT   Confédération Française Démocratique du Travail (French Democratic Labor Confederation)

CGT   Confédération Générale du Travail (General Labor Confederation)

EDF   Électricité de France (French Electric Authority)

FEN   Fédération de l'Éducation Nationale (National Education Federation)

FGA   Fédération Gauche Alternative (Alternative Left Federation, or Maoists)

FN   Front National (National Front)

GE   Génération Écologie (Ecology Generation)

LCR   Ligue Communiste Revolutionnaire (Revolutionary Communist League, or Trotskyists)

MEI   Mouvement Écologique Indépendent (Independent Ecological Movement)

MEP   Mouvement d'Écologie Politique (Political Ecology Movement)

PCF   Parti Communiste Français (French Communist Party)

PS   Parti Socialiste (Socialist Party)

PSU   Parti Socialiste Unifié (Unified Socialist Party)

RAT   Réseaux des Amis de la Terre (Network of Friends of the Earth)

RPR   Rassemblement pour la République (Rally for the Republic, or Gaullist Party)

SFIO   Section Française de l'Internationale Ouvrière (French Section of the Workers' International, or French Socialist Party before 1969)

UDF   Union pour la Démocratie Française (Union for French Democracy, or centrist bloc)

Germany

AL   Alternative Liste (Alternative List)

AUD   Aktionsgemeinschaft Unabhängiger Deutscher (Action Community of Independent Germans)

BBU   Bundesverband Bürgerinitiativen Umweltschultz (Federal Association of Citizens' Initiatives for Environmental Protection)

BI   Bürgeriniativen (Citizens' Initiative)

BL   Bunte List (Rainbow List)

CDU   Christliche-Demokratische Union (Christian Democratic Union)

CSU   Christliche-Soziale Union (Christian Social Union, Bavarian Christian Democrats)

FDP   Freie Demokratische Partei (Free Democratic Party)

KB   Kommunischer Bund (Communist Federation)

KPD   Kommuniste Partei Deutschland (German Communist Party)

GAL   Grüne Alternative Liste (Green Alternative List)

GAZ   Grüne Aktion Zukunft (Green Action Future)

GLSH   Grüne Liste Schleswig-Holstein (Green List of Schleswig-Holstein)

ÖDP   Ökologisch-Demokratische Partei (Ecological Democratic Party)

SPD   Sozialistik Partei Deutschlands (Social Democratic Party)

USP   Umweltschutzpartei (Environmental Protection Party)

Europe

ALÖ   Alternative Liste Österreichs (Austrian Alternative List)

PvdA   Partij van der Arbeit (Dutch Labor Party)

PCI   Partito Comunista Italiano (Italian Communist Party)

PS   Parti Socialiste (Socialist Party, Belgium, Francophone Region)

SAP   Sveriges Socialdemokratiska Abetarepartei (Swedish Social Democratic Party)

SP   Socialistische Partij (Socialist Party, Belgium, Flemish Region)

SPÖ   Sozialdemokratische Partei Österreichs (Austrian Social Democratic Party)

VGÖ   Vereinte Grünen Österreichs (Austrian United Greens)

Chapter One

Introduction: Competition and Change in Progressive Parties

Les Verts and *Die Grünen*: Contrasting Directions in Green Politics

When they first began to contest elections, it was clear to all that green parties were different. Their politics was "antipolitics." They formed on the crest of a wave of protest movements, claiming to be their heirs. These movements were initiated by student revolts and the mobilization of the independent New Left during the late 1960s and early 1970s, fed by trade union militancy during the 1970s, and crowned by antinuclear, peace and feminist movements toward the end of that decade. The greens maintained that their fundamental allegiance was with these new social movements, and not with the parliamentary institutions of which they were formally a part. They were beholden to neither the Right nor the Left: their programs called into question the entire apparatus of material growth and international security over which the parties of the Left and Right fought to become the managers. The greens have

1

since transformed their milieu by infusing environmental and other postindustrial themes into mainstream political discourse.

Yet we still do not know what makes green parties different from each other. Two major Western European ecology parties, *Les Verts* in France, and *Die Grünen* in the Federal Republic of Germany, moved in separate directions in a key domain, that of ideology. The parties' programmatic demands, and the fundamental assumptions about the nature of a just society that underlay them, diverged in significant ways. Different ideologies in turn implied different strategies. The *Grünen* and *Verts* had contrasting ideas about their own role in politics, and made distinct choices of allies and adversaries.

The crux of the distinction between the two parties lay in their view of the bridges to be built between the environmental and the social. The *Grünen*, a model for other green parties and for theories about them, advanced a left-wing version of political ecology.[1] They incorporated environmentalist themes into a comprehensive critique of capitalist society. They tried to elicit the support of economically disadvantaged social groups and trade unions, and aimed to reorganize the entire system of material production in the Federal Republic. The *Verts*, barely studied in this country, employed a strategy that is also poorly understood. It was radical, yet deliberately non-Marxist. The *Verts* insisted that the environmental crisis, and not class conflict, must be the key to understanding all other questions. Corresponding to this, their social goal has been to advance global decentralization and popular participation, and they see cultural minorities or inhabitants of natural regions as their natural allies or constituents. We refer to the German Greens' strategy as "red/green" or ecosocialist, and the *Verts*' as an ecoanarchist, or "pure ecological" type of program.[2] These strategic profiles hold for the period from 1980 to 1991 for the *Grünen* and 1986 to 1993 for the *Verts*.[3]

The European Greens have their origins in a reaction to problems in parliamentary socialist parties, and remain in their political orbit. Literature on postindustrial parties and movements notes that they tend to form in reaction to hierarchic tendencies in and political compromises of socialist or social democratic parties.[4] We take another step, placing the phenomenon in comparative perspective, and analyzing the patterns of interaction between the two. Green parties face Left when they frame their ideas and form their identities—even, perhaps most of all, those that insist that they are not of the Left. The greens in our two cases, however, confronted two different Lefts, and there were distinct axes of conflict. In the Federal Republic, the greens faced a conservative socialist party in a state of decline: the *Sozialdemokratische Partei Deutschlands* (SPD).[5] When the SPD settled on a progrowth, neoliberal response to a contracting economy, the *Grünen* moved to frame environmental demands in terms of themes the SPD had marginalized or suppressed, such as worker autonomy, major redistributive measures, or employment programs. In France, the greens faced a more formidable opponent. At around the same time, *Parti Socialiste Français* (PS) commanded most of the electoral resources of the French Left, and coopted the postindustrial themes of the Greens and the New Left that the SPD shunned.[6] Consigned to political irrelevance for years, the *Verts* finally advanced by evoking the environmental movement as the symbol of popular aspirations and grassroots democracy, thus distancing themselves from the centralist tendencies of the French Left.

In the end, red and green may be enmeshed in a common predicament. While each party's strategy has advantages that respond to its situation, each choice implies certain characteristic tradeoffs. It is not just the contrasting strategies, but the limits and paradoxes that may be inherent in each one, that this book seeks to understand.[7] Having distanced itself from the orthodoxy of the Third International and from the Soviet model, the contemporary Left—socialists, the greens and other alternative movements, and even communists—now tend to acknowledge the pluralism of complex modern societies. Indeed, while the progressive political field remains this fragmented, the notion of a plurality of goals may necessarily be elevated to a virtue. Yet the commitment to diversity comes into conflict with another essential one for the Left, both modern and postmodern: its identification with some privileged cause and the image of emancipation built around it. The Left's representatives originally derive their legitimacy from movements of alienated social actors with intense demands for change, for whom they claim to act. There is a tension between the need to stress a particular set of demands intensely, and the need to address a range of demands.

Burke grasped the problem in his remarks on the lofty aims and unjust acts of the French Revolution. To elevate any one set of demands to the status of an absolute and overriding moral premium must come into conflict with the complexity and moral ambiguity of any society as a whole. Yet Burke's corresponding prescription for incrementalism hardly puts the problem to rest, as the history of social democracy might suggest. Socialist parties in the late nineteenth and early twentieth century had to address the class interests of industrial workers, while still securing the interclass solidarity needed to attain electoral majorities.[8] They tried to embrace political diversity, and the parliamentary institutions that foster it, while still pressing for significant change. The vague commitment to liberal rights and institutions, and the economic interests of a broad class of citizens has, with time, become associated with a loss of momentum toward change. We shall refer to the fundamental dilemma as one of "identity" versus "efficacy." The pure ecological and red/green strategies, respectively, may represent the opposed sides of this dilemma.

The underlying instability in each strategy is simply aggravated today by intramural competition within the Left, whether between socialists and communists or greens and socialists, since the limits of one strategy are corresponding opportunities for another party. Over time, individual parties may oscillate between identity and efficacy as they try to respond to their adversaries' moves or the tensions in their own choices. To account for these dynamics, we construct a model of strategic interaction based on the mutual positioning and characteristic tradeoffs in green/socialist competition in France and Germany. To suggest why such a model is needed, let us consider alternate approaches for explaining the ideologies and strategies of progressive parties.

Toward a Model of Strategic Interaction

To account for the ideological variation in German and French ecology parties, we might begin by examining their countries' cultural paradigms. As with any unalloyed culturalist formulation, however, there is a great deal of history that does not fit. French culture, supposedly antagonistic to the natural world, produced a lively environmental movement, and a more holistic, "deep ecological" image of green politics.[9] And Germany, known for its reactionary forest mythology, gave rise to a profoundly social constructionist and progressive variant of ecology.[10]

A wealth of recent literature suggests that ideas exist in symbiosis with political institutions.[11] Where the greens stand might be linked to where they sit within the matrix of national political institutions. French institutions are rather centralized, for example, compared to those of the Federal Republic. It may not be suprising, then, that demands for political decentralization take a more important place in the *Verts'* ideas than in those of the *Grünen*. Still, it is hard to fully explain the substantive differences in each party's programmatic agendas with reference to the institutional structure of either country. Both favored decentralization of some kind—but why did one emphasize the benefits to the environment, while the other foresaw premiums of social justice and the reorganization of work? It is true that West Germany has an enormous and well-organized working class—but portions of it were quite conservative, and little inclined to support an initiative to transform the economy in an ecosocialist direction.

Recent literature on ecology parties deal with more immediate features of the green parties' political environment, such as the preferences of their typical electorate, or the political situation they confront. Inglehart, for example, holds that ecology parties form to represent "postmaterial values," which in turn reflect changes in the occupational structure of advanced societies and the concerns of the generation born after World War II.[12] Kitschelt groups ecology parties within a larger category of "left-libertarian" parties that advocate decentralized politics along with egalitarian reforms, and notes their response to external opportunities and constraints, such as their relative electoral competitiveness or the attitude of elites toward their demands.[13]

The problem in these analyses is that parties move within a predefined space in the party system along a single unilinear ideological scale. Party ideology is thus assumed rather than explained. That preempts the possibility that otherwise comparable parties such as the French and German Greens would advance substantively different ideologies. Why were the *Grünen* as much materialist as postmaterialist? Why were the *Verts* more libertarian than left?

We cannot solve this problem by referring to the position of potential competitors within this space. If both socialist parties allowed a "space" to open up that the greens then moved to fill, how is it that they filled it with different programmatic material? If the French Socialist Party was more successful than North European social democratic parties at coopting postmaterial or libertarian demands advanced by the French New Left, why did the *Verts* turn out to be the more postmaterial of the two in response? By the same token, it does not help to introduce additional competitors, and thus bilateral or multilateral competition into the equation. That would assume that parties as different as communist parties, at one end of the spectrum, and centrist liberal parties at the other, compete with greens and socialists on the basis of some clearly defined, single issue or set of issues for an identifiable electorate, which is not likely. We are not so omniscient that we know precisely what the crux of competition will be in advance.

Kitschelt's and Inglehart's unilinear scales also assume that some unique equilibrium is possible in which each party's strength and position adequately reflects the level of support for a given programmatic stance. The situation is actually far more unstable. Each strategy, even a successful one, has certain limitations that should become more pronounced the more the party holds fast to it. As tension mounts, adversaries may profit from defections. We do not seek equilibria, then, but a more dynamic model that can account for the unfolding consequences of any given strategy, and the parties' mutual interaction.

We propose to go beyond a single spatial dimension and consider the possibility that two distinct and contradictory rationalities govern the parties' strategies, shaping the ideological material available to them. On one side stands identity, on the other, efficacy. To move in the direction of identity, the party stresses the demands of a distinct movement constituency. To move toward efficacy, the party represents the widest possible range of causes or bases of support. The first tendency seeks to shore up the most intense and reliable support for change; the second tries to assemble the largest numbers to effect change. One implies doctrinal purity and autonomy, with the aim of portraying the party as the sole legitimate representative of a given cause. The other seeks points of programmatic convergence, in the name of forging alliances, either in a diverse coalition supporting the party, or with forces outside the party. Attributes of identity and efficacy may overlap in any given party strategy, since all will try to reconcile the two imperatives. Yet the more they are combined, the more we should expect to observe tension mount between ideological purity and ideological range, between core commitment and coalition.

When two progressive parties compete, it is rational for them to move toward opposite sides of this tradeoff. Socialist parties, as parties of government, tend toward efficacy. The challengers should therefore have to maximize identity in order to present themselves as a clear alternative. When they lead or participate in government, socialist parties risk major threats to their identity. The SPD's management of a powerful industrial economy brought it into conflict with its traditional identity as the representative of the German working class, to a point where it could satisfy neither goal. While the SPD had a weak identity, and poor efficacy as well, the *Grünen* could fuse red and green symbolism without any danger to their own identity. Where attributes of identity and efficacy coexist in a single party, it is both politically powerful and oriented toward major reform. Thus the political space for alternative progressive parties is severely curtailed. The French Socialist Party, for example, came to power with a strikingly radical economic program, supported by a diverse coalition of progressive and left-wing forces. In that situation, the French ecologists faced strong obstacles, but they benefited from stressing identity—that is, the purity and distinctiveness of ecology—even more intensely than their German analogues did. No strategy is without tensions, as we have insisted, and a party like the PS that maximizes both may experience the strongest backlash. As the Socialist's coalition bent under the strains of holding power, the French Greens would interpret the PS's power itself, and the socialist doctrine that undergirded it, as a political liability. The limits in the greens' own strategic choices will not go unnoticed: centrifugal forces among factions in the *Grünen* would strain its identity; whereas the *Verts* had difficulty transcending the pure green identity they constructed for themselves.

Plan of the Book

The next chapter introduces the main events and actors in our empirical study, and structures the comparison between them. We consider the ways that intellectual and political history, administrative and parliamentary institutions, and social and electoral trends might have shaped the greens' strategies. We argue that the crucial point of contrast is in the character and strength of social democracy in each country. The German industrial working class was traditionally well organized, and, by the postwar period, well integrated in the political economic regime. In France, the trade union movement has been politically divided and often antagonistic to the regime. Yet when global recession and the growth of the New Left posed strong challenges to the social democratic model that the SPD embodied, weak social democracy meant strong socialism (incarnated in the politically flexible, "modern" PS in France). That, in turn, would leave its mark on the nascent alternative movements which had initially mobilized in support of the PS and SPD, and later on the ecology parties that sought to present a more progressive alternative to them.

Chapter 3 develops a framework for analyzing the interaction between socialist and green parties. Two sets of theoretical literature speak to our concerns: works on the new social movements that inspired and supported green politics,[14] and those on parties and party systems.[15] Despite different political emphases, the two literatures both stress the importance of ideas and ideologies in political strategies. After taking note of their complementary perspectives, we try to synthesize them. Our model notes the strategic tradeoffs progressive parties face between the goals of movements and the imperatives of parties, and attempts to explain when and why they choose identity over efficacy, or vice versa.

In chapter 4, we look at politics inside the *Grünen* and *Verts*. An extremely diverse set of perspectives on the nature and aims of the environmental movement coexisted uneasily within these organizations. Our problem is therefore to ask how these competing perspectives can ever translate into coherent, competitive strategies. We refer to a seminal work on the subject: Herbert Kitschelt's *Logics of Party Formation*. Kitschelt explains the greens' strategies in terms of changes in their internal coalitions and corresponding changes in the set of external opportunities and constraints. In light of our application of Kitschelt's framework to a new case, that of *Les Verts*, we argue that Kitschelt's analysis does not focus sufficiently on the variations in ideological goals among characteristic factions, nor on ideological competition between established parties of the Left and ecology parties.

In chapter 5, we interpret the ideas behind the contrasting ecological strategies. Drawing from the *Grünen's* and *Verts'* campaign programs, internal party documents, and leaders' political statements or writings, we try to uncover the basic assumptions and priorites informing each one. The *Grünen's* red/green program emphasizes the material side of ecological questions, centering on the social and enviromental consequences of industrial production. The *Verts'* focuses on the procedural side, highlighting the benefits of greater individual and regional autonomy, and the types of institutions that facilitate them. We discuss the parties' views of problems in market economics, the central state, and the corresponding models of ecologically and socially just societies they advance as an alternative in light of these contrasting emphases. We intend the chapter as a contribution to work exploring the intrinsic differences between the ecosocialist and ecoanarchist worldviews—though the programs are all the more significant in that they were formed and tested in practice as the greens established themselves during the last decade and a half.

The next four chapters focus on the dynamics of competition between the ecologists and socialists and the strategic tradeoffs each party has made. Each one of these chapters discusses a characteristic phase in the greens' development. In chapter 6, the status of the socialist party (i.e., the SPD in crisis, the PS on the ascendant) structures the green's strategic options and shapes their identities even as they begin to form out of a heterogenous set of electoral lists or prototype parties. In chapter 7, the strategies undergo major tests, and major successes determine the red/green and pure green directions afterward. In chapter 8, the ecologists begin to build a stable core of electoral support around their respective strategies, while signs of the inherent limits in each one start to appear. The *Verts* built their identity very carefully around the themes of the environmental movement, but they lacked credibility when they tried to broaden their alternative program to include other issues. Further, their strategy of strict autonomy from other parties put them in a morally ambiguous position on the issue of alliances to thwart the progress of the *Front National* (FN), France's anti-immigrant party. The *Grünen's* red/green strategy leaned more toward efficacy than a clear identity. They tried to rally a diverse social constituency around opposition to capitalist industrial production.Yet that undermined their ability to define their identity when the socialist party changed its own strategy to accommodate green and postindustrial issues.

Chapter 9 compares two major national elections in France and Germany in which the limitations of each strategy manifest themselves, leading to severe setbacks in each case. The resulting crises within the parties in turn paved the way to a change of leadership, and with that, a change in strategy. Each one now shows signs of moving toward the other's earlier position—the *Grünen* toward a pure green profile and the *Verts* even more clearly toward red/green. We argue that that, too, should be explained in terms of major strategic changes in the status of the leading Center-Left party. The final section of chapter 9 applies this framework to green/socialist relations in six other Western European countries: Britain, Austria, Belgium, Sweden, the Netherlands, and Italy.

In our Conclusion, we discuss some significant new developments in green politics in France and Germany, and the two parties' prospects for the future, in light of our framework. Representatives of both parties are either members of the national government or are expected to be in the near future. The *Grünen* have made themselves the third strongest political force in Germany, and are poised to form the next government in Bonn. The *Verts* have finally entered the French National Assembly after trying for thirteen years, and placed one of their own, Dominique Voynet, in the current Socialist Government as Minister for the Environment and Regional Policy. We conclude that it is still in the greens' interest to emphasize the greens' distinct identity vis-à-vis mainstream socialist politics, and that these tentative moves toward coalition risk damaging this identity. We also ask whether the competing rationalities of identity and efficacy are relevant to other areas of study, such as the politics of European integration, transitions to democracy, or the new nationalism and xenophobic politics.

Chapter *Two*

The Greens in Comparative Historical Perspective: From Social Democracy to Ecology

Introduction: Green Politics—a Case of "German Exceptionalism"?

Most work on ecological politics tends to view the Federal Republic as its epicenter.[1] It is clear that many features of postwar German politics combined to make ecology a central issue there during the 1980s: rapid postwar industrial growth; a youth movement alienated by this process, and by the country's failure to atone for its troubled past; and a decentralized political system within which environmental protest could easily find expression. The *Grünen*'s pathbreaking entry into the *Bundestag*, Germany's national parliament, in 1983 lent force to the idea that ecology was an essential aspect of its national destiny. Yet France also possesed some of the social conditions, protest movements, and facilitating institutions to set the political bedrock for green politics, and the latter made its impact felt there only several years later. Green politics in France may therefore be just as significant as the better-known German model.

In the movements that anticipated the French and German Greens' themes, in their motives for forming parties, and in their leadership, organizational dynamics, and social base, there are, in fact, many parallels. A single feature of the greens' milieu, however, stands out in contrast. That is the organization and strength of the leading party of the Left: firmly rooted but declining in Germany; rising and politically hegemonic in France. As the New Left began to question more established forms of working-class or left-wing politics, the PS met the challenge successfully, whereas the more phlegmatic SPD foundered. By establishing this crucial contrast here, we can suggest in later chapters the ways that competition with the socialists shaped the greens' self-understanding in distinctive ways, and set them on different strategic routes to comparable levels of impact and influence.

Environmentalism, the Left and the New Left in Historical Perspective: Institutional and Political Factors

Germany's relatively decentralized institutions and politics facilitated environmental protection and favored the movements based on it. Though hardly free from environmental degradation or controversy surrounding it, Germany had had a fairly enlightened policy toward the environment as early as the nineteenth century, when preunification German *Länder* (states) and private business associations regulated water and air pollution. In this century, after World War II, a premium on strict adherence to legal principles set by the institutions of the Federal Republic has fostered precautionary and preventive attitudes toward potential environmental hazards.[2] In the 1970s, German citizens were moved to act on a range of public policy issues, spawning a movement known as the *Burgerinitiativen* (BIs), and their concerns often centered on environmental problems and the nuclear power program. Finally, Germany's dependent geopolitical status left it beholden to the U.S. and NATOs prerogatives in the matter of nuclear armaments, and that aroused hostility among the German public. In Germany, then, the *Grünen* arrived in the political arena with a readily available discourse about environmentalism and gained momentum from broadly based public support.

Though it has had an influential environmental movement for more than a hundred years, France's centralized institutions often prevented significant action to protect the environment at all but a local level. In the postwar period, environmental organizations were coopted by the state, through funding and supervision. Elites charged with regional or energy policy were insulated from public opposition, since there were few legal and political channels for airing grievances. General DeGaulle, jealous of France's autonomy, supported a massive nuclear energy program and independent nuclear arsenal. In the early 1980s, the French nuclear program gained the support of the leaders of the political Left, as well as those of the Right, throttling an antinuclear movement that had raged for a decade.[3] Nevertheless, the antinuclear movement left a reserve of popular sympathy and awareness. Away from Paris, where suburban decay and large student populations elicit support for green issues, the *Verts* had their best scores in areas where there were significant protests over local nuclear deployment. Further, when the antinuclear initiative failed, activists in the provinces turned to other areas, such as species preservation, wilderness and resource protection, or developing alternative forms of energy, and thus helped sustain some of the momentum and local visibility of the French environmental movement. Networks of environmental and antinuclear protest organization established during the 1970s and 1980s helped support the green party's candidates and issues later, much as the citizens' initiatives did in West Germany.[4]

The legacy of German militarism may have left traces on the *Grünen*'s red/green worldview. With conservative intellectual traditions discredited, Marxism and socialism held a strong attraction for German intellectuals and academics after World War II, and well into the 1980s.[5] (Marxist ideas and the Soviet model lost the aura they had once had among French intellectuals with the revelations of the atrocities of the Gulag in the mid-1970s.) Further, the need to prevent further upheavals of the kind caused by National Socialism, and the exigencies of West German reconstruction, gave rise to a highly conservative regime—and a left-wing discourse of opposition to it. Regarding foreign policy, German expansionism would be checked, of course, by Germany's division into two parts and its weak and dependent position in the geopolitical arena. In the domestic arena, the Federal Republic's constitution of 1949, the Basic Law, gave political parties a formal role. Yet parties or individuals deemed subversive to the democratic order could be barred from meaningful participation. The constitutional court outlawed the *Kommunistiche Partei Deutschlands* (KPD) in 1956—and thus there would be no organization in the party system to the Left of the Social Democrats. In 1972, the SPD, sponsored legislation prohibiting radicals from civil service employment, and many suspected leftists were screened out. Since it thus had no effective political representation, the German alternative Left, which comprised student radicals or disaffected intellectuals, developed a highly ghettoized and antinomian political culture that was inclined toward Marxist discourse about the environmental and social detriments of capitalism, and sympathetic to "actual existing socialism" in the East. The association of all mainstream parties with this conservative regime gave rise in the years immediately following the war to a movement that acted wholly outside of formal institutions, the Extraparliamentary Opposition, whose grassroots organizational style and opposition to rearmament and nuclear power the *Grünen* would try to revive later.[6]

The radicalism of the German Left was embodied, in its most extreme form, in the paramilitary tactics and violence of the Red Army Faction during the 1970s. Opposition to the postwar regime emerged in only slightly less radical form in a multitude of Leninist and Maoist splinter groups, many of whose members were later active in the *Grünen*. During the same period, France did not lack militant cadres with a socialist orientation, nor a wider left-wing opposition to the regime, nor activists who travelled from this milieu to the *Verts* later. But in France, members of this opposition either supported the Socialist Party in its path to power, or were simply eclipsed by its rise. Thus, while there were similarities in the attitudes and background of members of the independent or alternative Left in France and Germany, the political circumstances they faced, precisely as the greens were forming, were extremely different. This is the story we need to tell to understand the difference in the ecology parties' outlooks.

The Socialist Left in Germany and France:
Multiple Contradictions of Social Democracy

The SPD and the PS were creatures of and integral parts of their institutional regimes. As such, both were potential targets for opposition from their Left. The German Social Democratic Party played a pivotal role in German reconstruction after 1945, having led an industrial working class with growing rates of unionization since the end of the last century. After World War II, this linkage helped secure industrial peace, in exchange for which workers received substantial redistributive benefits as individuals and unions gained a significant (though still junior) role on management boards. Recognizing the need to recapture the political Center, the SPD formally renounced an earlier commitment to socialism at the Bad Godesberg conference in 1958. That shift in strategy ultimately allowed it to enter into the government in Bonn with the formation of the Grand Coalition, which joined the SPD with both the centrist *Freie Demokratische Partei* (FDP) and the Christian Democratic parties (the *Christliche-Demokratische Union*, or CDU, and the *Christliche-Soziale Union*, or CSU) in 1966. After 1969, the SPD led a coalition with the FDP from 1969 to 1982.

The *Parti Socialiste* also emerged as a party of government during the postwar era, though it would gain power for the first time fourteen years later than the SPD. The commanding figure in that period had been Charles De Gaulle, who shaped the Fifth Republic, instituted in 1958, to his liking. Like other modernizing French leaders, DeGaulle favored a centralized administrative apparatus and a highly autonomous executive power. In the Gaullist conception, the state would serve as a neutral arbiter among competing interests in what was at that time still a regionally underdeveloped and politically polarized society. The Gaullist myth of the monarchical presidency imbued that office with a degree of power rare in Europe. Directly elected by universal suffrage for a seven-year term, the president may claim to stand above the fray of partisan conflict. French parties needed to tender an electable candidate for the office, and those without one suffered in influence.[7] In foreign policy, De Gaulle's strategy had been to assert France's prerogatives within the context of global superpower rivalry. Thus France tried to maintain its own sphere of influence in the Third World, as well to build an independent defense capability linked to a program of nuclear energy, contrasting Germany's highly dependent status.

The Socialist Party was, in many ways, the Left's answer to Gaullism. The majoritarian ballot system in presidential and parliamentary elections, intended to counter the fragmentation and instability of the Fourth Republic, threw votes and seats to the largest and most viable government party on either side of the political spectrum, rather than to less established challengers. Commanding a broad segment of moderate to left-leaning voters, the PS gradually benefited at the expense of the *Parti Communiste Français* (PCF), the New Left *Parti Socialiste Unifié* (PSU), and, later, the ecologists. Its leader, François Mitterrand, showed flexible political convictions and great skill in orchestrating French political infighting. Mitterrand had mounted a promising campaign against DeGaulle in the presidential elections of 1965. When in office after 1981, he became a convert to some of the Gaullist regime's most centralized institutional features.

In power, the PS might have become implicated with the state's more authoritarian or conservative features, clearly a problem for the SPD vis-a-vis its own Left. Yet the *Parti Socialiste* managed to negotiate the twin challenges of opposition from its Left, and the global turn toward neoliberal economics, all of which would hasten the SPD's fall from power. The PS's internal organization and relations with supporting social groups or organizations gave it a political flexibility the SPD did not possess.[8] Unlike the SPD and many North European social democratic parties, the PS had no clear ties to a unified trade movement. Reorganized in 1969 and placed firmly under Mitterrand's control in 1971, France's new Socialist Party was by design a campaign machine for its leaders and a viable party of government. Neither the former incarnation, the *Section Française de l'Internationale Ouvrière* (SFIO), nor the PCF, had been able to combine both attributes. The party consisted of career politicians, almost all of whom were members of the middle class in intellectual professions. If social diversity was limited, there was ideological diversity. Elections to the PS's governing bodies were tied to votes on programmatic motions at party congresses, and positions were allotted by proportional representation. Each one of the sharply defined ideological factions that resulted from this system—whether left-wing socialist, reformist, or New Left—was to play a tactical role whenever shifts in circumstances made it expedient for the PS to show one political face or another.[9] As we shall suggest, there was irony in the fact that the PS could effectively respond to the demands of a diverse set of constituents by virtue of its relative autonomy from any one in particular.

The SPD, founded in 1896, evolved as a bureaucratic mass party, not a party of leaders like the PS. Its relatively hierarchic organization allowed few prospects for left-wing members to advance to the party's highest echelons. Though there was sharp factional conflict between the party's Left and Right during the 1970s, the dispute failed to change the basic direction of the SPD. Its factions were informal tendencies, not organized groups with a specific party function as in the PS. The predominant faction was the Right, whose members were either former manual workers with an authoritarian outlook, such as Holger Börner, other leaders with a populist touch such as Johannes Rau, or technocrats sympathetic to the party's working-class constituency, such as Helmut Schmidt.[10]

The PS's center of gravity was thus far to the Left of that of the SPD during the same period. In 1969, when the party was reorganized from the more moderate SFIO, the Socialists formally committed themselves to a strategy of Union of the Left with the Communist Party. Mitterrand explicitly aimed to outflank the PCF, and the benefits of the allied strategy would indeed flow to his party later on. Further the PS/PCF Common Program, signed in 1972, incorporated New Left themes: such as demands for worker's control and decentralized forms of production known as *autogestion*, or self-management, which had been a rallying cry since the student uprisings of May 1968. By the middle of the decade, there were initiatives to enhance ties between the PS and the trade union movment, which the PCF possessed and the SFIO had lacked. The ideological ferment of these years crystallized in the *Projet Socialiste de la France des années 80* (French Socialist Project for the 1980s), a strikingly radical program of nationalizations and fiscal intervention the PS advanced when it won the presidency and parliamentary majority a year later.

The SPD chose a far more moderate course. Helmut Schmidt, Chancellor after 1974, aimed to shore up German competitiveness in the face of global inflation, and thus turned to austerity and monetary discipline. He regarded that as the best way to further the interests of the party's working-class membership and electoral base in the long run. But unions grew restive toward the end of the decade, engaging in rare strike actions. At the same time, the SPD's status as a government party had pushed it ever further away from the independent socialist Left or the popular movements of the day—i.e., from the peace movement during the 1950s, from the Extraparliamentary Opposition of the 1960s, from its own youth wing in the 1970s, and from the *Grünen* in the 1980s.

The PS, like the SPD, eventually acted against the interests of its working-class constituency after only a year in power. The PS's notorious "U-turn" commenced in 1982, when the party shifted away from planning and economic nationalism of the *Projet Socialiste* toward fiscal austerity and monetary rigor. Yet it was insulated from trade union vetos of its restructuring program, and that freed it to focus on other initiatives that centrist or center-left voters might support. The PCF, which had withdrawn its ministers from the PS government by mid-1984, articulated some of the hostility felt by the most threatened sectors, such as the steel and coal industries and by the *Confédération Générale du Travail* (CGT) the Communist-controlled union federation. Yet the PCF's shrinking social base and perennial tactical errors meant that it would not gain to the point of becoming a threat to the PS.[11]

While stemming a challenge from the Old Left represented by the Communists and their allies in the trade unions, the PS also held the support of the New Left and the relatively young, new middle-class segment of the electorate. The PS had actually failed to deliver on some of its promises to New Left organizations that had been an integral part of the coalition that brought it to power. These promises had included a stronger role for trade unions in industrial relations, particularly for New Left-oriented public sector union, the *Confédération Française Démocratique du Travail* (CFDT), and a moratorium on nuclear power sought by the environmentalists. Despite these reversals, the PS maintained a reserve of political trust with a wider circle of progressive voters. This was particularly true in the area of liberalization and democratization of government and industry, which became central elements of the PS's strategy after its forced retreat from its left-leaning economic program. Reforms that echoed certain New Left themes were transmuted into articles of government—i.e., decentralization (the Defferre Laws of 1982) and worker self-management (the Auroux Laws of 1984). The Socialists also brought representatives of the New Left into their first governments: former PSU head Huguette Bouchardeau became Secretary for the Environment, and a prominent feminist, Yvette Roudy, headed the Ministry for Women's Rights. Finally, Mitterrand made it a priority to liberalize the French justice system, and used this as a plank against the right-wing cabinet, which regained the National Assembly from 1986 to 1988.[12]

At the beginning of the 1970s, in the aftermath of the student protest movement, both socialist parties had tried to kindle the energies of the youth movement to support party organizing and campaigning and help them take on a "modern" image. Both saw a huge influx of new members.[13] Yet, as we have seen, their issues were embraced by important currents in the PS as it gradually rose to power, whereas SPD leaders strongly resisted any accommodation to them. After the protests of 1968, many German student leftists joined the Jusos ("Young Socialists"), an SPD party association meant to provide a forum for young people. The Jusos pressed a radical agenda: withdrawal from NATO, political decentralization, inclusion of women, and attention to a cause that had only just begun to claim the attention of progressives in West Germany, the environment. Sensing a threat to the party's stability, the leadership moved to bar the Jusos from the advancement through the party hierarchy they duly expected. The squabbles had brought bad publicity, distracted leaders from other matters, and cost the party many members. Since the right wing had prevailed after about 1977, the party's internal politics were at least more stable, for the time being. Yet that in turn bred stasis, preventing the organization from responding to a greater challenge: the rise of a new party to its Left—the *Grünen*—and the issues they advanced.

The SPD maintained its careful, centrist outlook in spite of obvious signals that there was a young, progressive, and green current in its own electorate. In Federal and *Landtag* (state parliament) elections of 1978–1980, their votes flowed from the SPD and FDP to the newly formed *Grünen*.[14] Massive popular mobilizations against NATO missile deployment between 1979 and 1983 might also have indicated the broadly based support for issues the Greens were beginning to articulate. The SPD's excessive

caution led it to misinterpret an extremely explosive issue that
followed: NATO's twin-track decision reserving its prerogative to
station Pershing missiles on German soil, pending the outcome of
further superpower negotiations, without consultation with German authorities. In the 1983 campaign for the *Bundestag*, chancellor candidate Hans-Jochen Vogel avoided taking either an
anti-Soviet, pro-Western position, or the pacifist position of the
Greens, feeding the latter's striking breakthrough in that election.[15] Further, the SPD resisted concessions on nuclear power,
despite strong popular opposition, until 1986. The SPD leadership's inability to fully appreciate the significance of the rise of
the Greens and the new politics contributed to the fall of its government in 1982, and to its subsequent loss in the parliamentary
elections of 1983 and 1987.

Ultimately, the PS was not invincible, and in its strengths lay
the seeds of its downfall. The party could not sustain its claim to
be a progressive force while manifestly preserving its autonomy
from any core constituency. It had no reliable base of popular support, working-class or other, to fall back on. That was especially
critical after a series of broken promises, rising unemployment,
and the party's increasingly technocratic profile wore away its image as a dynamic force for change. Further, due to the PS's elitist
format, its leaders wound up quarrelling over the palace while the
kingdom decayed. Internal PS factions, once a source of flexibility,
became a political deadweight and an obstacle to change.[16] Programmatic motions eventually turned into sheer leadership tests,
and the stakes were no longer ideological but purely political (e.g.,
the conquest of the presidency after Mitterrand, or control over
the PS itself). Power struggles flared at the Toulouse Congress in
1985, and once again at the Rennes Congress of 1990, signifying
to party activists and voters alike that the party leaders were pri-
marily concerned with their own power.[17] Having betrayed the
progressive movements it once rallied in the name of broad electoral efficacy, the Socialists were to bear the full consequences in
the elections at the beginning of the 1990s.

Furthermore, the SPD, though conservative, was not mono-
lithic. A cohort of younger, more green-minded SPD leaders were
building political bases in the *Länder*, and then finally rose to key
party positions toward the end of the 1980s. These were Oskar
Lafontaine (minister-president of the Saarland and chancellor

candidate in 1990); Gerhard Schröder (minister-president of Lower Saxony); and Björn Engholm (minister-president of Schleswig-Holstein; party chairman in 1990–1993 and then presumed chancellor candidate). Like many Greens, these younger SPD leaders entered politics as student organizers or Jusos (of which Schröder, for example, had once been chairman). By the mid-1980s, they had moved far closer to a neoliberal position on economic issues than most members of the Greens. Yet their cultural liberalism, and particularly their sensitivity to the new environmental awareness in the German public, put these SPD modernizers much closer than their predecessors to the *Grünen*'s outlook. That had significant effects on the latter's ability to project an identity as the sole voice for environmental demands in Germany.

The Rise, Decline, and Resurgence of the German and French Green Parties: From Environmentalism to Ecology

New Left activists and environmentalists who were present at the creation of the *Grünen* and *Verts* formed parties reluctantly.[18] Many of them had supported the SPD or PS earlier, either as militants or as voters, and were frustrated with the hierarchical tendencies they found in the established parties of the Left.[19] Their rationale in forming parties was that they had to achieve a more persistent form of pressure on the party system and wider dissemination of their ideas, though there was always internal strife surrounding the question as to how far the parties should go toward becoming an established part of their political system.

The environmental moved actually had an earlier start in organized politics in France. In 1973, Solange Fernex and Antoine Waechter, who would later represent the pure ecological line within the *Verts* formed one of Europe's first environmental parties, *Écologie et Survie*, in Alsace for the legislative elections in 1973. In 1974, Marxist agronomist René Dumont ran in the presidential elections on a platform of environmental themes, winning 1.34 percent of the vote, but raising awareness of the issues nonetheless. Environmental/Alternative Left fusion lists won thirty seats nationwide in French municipal elections in 1977. Brice Lalonde, a future Environment Minister, received 3.87 percent in the 1981 presidential elections that placed François Mitterrand in office. In West Germany, the turn toward electoral politics commenced later, but with immediate results: a fusion of alternative leftists, former SPD members, and centrist environmentalists scored 5.1 percent in Bremen in 1979, and ecologists entered a legislative body with significant regional power, a German *Land* parliament, for the first time. Given this momentum, permanent national parties formed shortly afterward. In France, the *Mouvement d'Écologie Politique* fused with the *Confédération Écologiste* after years of stalled negotiations, in January 1984, forming the party officially titled *Les Verts/Confédération Écologiste-Parti Écologiste*. In West Germany, *Die Grünen* formed from smaller ecological parties of diverse political origins in January 1980.

Although the *Grünen* obtained a disappointing 1.9 percent in the 1980 Federal election, successes in *Land* or city-state contests in the next two years gave the *Grünen* more seats in regional parliaments, and especially more publicity and stature, since they were taking votes away from the SPD and the FDP. In the 1983 Federal elections of 1983, they won 5.6 percent of the vote and 27 seats, bringing them international recognition. The *Grünen's* first major programmatic document, the *1980 Federal Program,* set the party's "red/green" programmatic agenda for the next decade. They entered the *Bundestag* in 1983, and returned in 1987 with 8.3 percent of the vote and forty-two seats, with the same strategy. These years saw further *Land* victories, some over 10 percent; membership in the party increased from around eighteen thousand to forty thousand; and a core electorate of about 60 percent of their vote began to support the *Grünen* reliably.[20] Along with these successes, however, the centrifugal forces of factional rivalry emerged in around 1982 that would strain the party to the point of crisis later. The party "realos" or realists favored winning immediate reforms through participation in governments with the SPD, whereas the "fundis" or fundamentalists saw the party as a propaganda arm of the extraparliamentary social movements and opposed any further movement toward convergence with other parties.

During the elections to the first all-German *Bundestag*, these divisions contributed to a striking reversal in the German ecology party's fortunes. The *Grünen* scored only 4.8 percent and thus won no seats. The ecological grouping in the *Länder* of the former

East Germany, *Bundnis '90* (Alliance '90), won 6.8 percent, with eight seats. But the *Grünen* had opposed the absorption of East German political parties by Western ones and thus refused to form a common slate with their Eastern counterparts. Since the debacle, both fundamentalists and some realists left the Grünen, the former to their own splinter groups, the latter to the SPD. A centrist current, which had called for factional reconciliation and calling itself *Aufbruch* ("new departure") first emerged in 1988, and then allied with remaining realists in 1991 to steer the party. After that point, the *Grünen* began to emphasize the environmental core of their program more strictly—a turn toward a pure ecological strategy.

The *Grünen* then began to rebound in regional and city-state elections. Their scores sometimes reached more than 10 percent, and they have participated in several *Land* Governments. In the elections to the Federal Parliament on October 16th, 1994, the *Grünen*, by then officially merged with the Greens of the former East Germany under the title *Bundnis '90/Die Grünen*, won 7.3 percent of the vote and reclaimed forty-nine seats. Antje Vollmer, a founding member of the Greens and an initiator of *Aufbruch*, was subsequently appointed a vice president of the *Bundestag*, another first for the ecology party. A party congress in December 1994 confirmed the predominance of the *Aufbruch* strategy, though a moderate left-wing current still exists. At this writing, polls show a majority of German voters prefer a Green/SPD coalition to the coalition of the Christian Democrats and the FDP now leading the country.

Despite its earlier start, French political ecology became a significant force in the French party system later than in Germany. After they formed in 1984, the *Verts'* scores were generally marginal. During this period the *Verts* were headed by a left-wing ecological current. This current included leaders Yves Cochet, once active in the student protests in 1968 and later in the CFDT, and Didier Anger, a veteran of the first wave of New Left activity since the 1950s and also active in the *Fédération de l'Éducation Nationale* (FEN). The left-ecological current also included Guy Hascoët and Pierre Radanne, who hailed from the Socialist-controlled Nord/Pas-de-Calais region.

The *Verts'* fortunes shifted when the party's internal majority changed in 1986.[21] From that point until late in 1993, the *Verts* advanced a pure ecological strategy, emphasizing the political and ideological distinctiveness of ecology. The winning majority was headed by Antoine Waechter, an environmental consultant by profession, and its ranks were filled mostly by activists whose political experience lay not in the universities or trade unions in Paris but in the grassroots environmental movement in the provinces. Waechter's austere, yet technically competent persona struck a chord with voters increasingly disenchanted with an increasingly scandal-ridden political class of the Right and Left. His score in the presidential elections of 1988, although only 3.7 percent, was striking for a man hitherto completely unknown to French voters. In the spring of 1989, the *Verts* also performed well in the municipals of March (8.1 percent where present, with 1,369 offices filled) and European Parliament elections in June (10.6 percent, with nine deputies—the party's highest independent score).

In France, the realist opposition to fundamentalism of the kind that Waechter represented resulted in the formation of a new party, *Génération Écologie*, by Brice Lalonde in 1990. GE's program, like the *Verts'*, focused on environmental demands, but its structure was more professionalized and its leadership far more pragmatic. In the next major contest, the regional elections of 1992, the *Verts* watched a sizable portion of their voters switch to GE. With 6.8 per cent going to the *Verts* and 7.2 to *GE*, the combined score was 14 percent—an indication of the ecology's new legitimacy in France. Further, the *Verts* saw one of their own, Marie-Christine Blandin, become president of the Nord/Pas-de-Calais region.[22] Yet the image of a movement rent by leadership feuds was extremely damaging to the *Verts*—and GE's success proved ephemeral at any rate.

Lalonde, the pragmatist, was so promiscuous in his choice of allies that he squandered his credibility as a "responsible" environmentalist upon whom the political class could depend. Thus in 1988, he entered the cabinet of PS Prime Minister Michel Rocard as Secretary, then Minister of the Environment. Lalonde formed an electoral pact with the *Verts* after the Socialists suffered a historic rout in the 1992 Regional elections. Within two years, he had petitioned to place GE in the center-right political federation, the *Union pour la Démocratie Française* (UDF), and GE was part of the presidential majority of Jacques Chirac in 1995 and 1997. Due to his patent desire to use GE for his personal gain and his drift toward the Right, Lalonde faced a rebellion within his own party in early 1994, and saw the defection of the rest of its leadership. Though he has regained control of GE, the party has never since scored more than 2 percent.

After its high water mark in the 1992 regionals, French ecology, by then severely fractured, entered a period of crisis and recomposition similar to that of the *Grünen* in 1990. In the March 1993 legislative elections, which saw an electoral pact between the *Verts* and *GE*, the two scored only 7.63 percent together, half their combined score a year before. In November 1993, the pure ecological current lost control of the *Verts* to the left-ecologists, who nevertheless had only a relative majority. Unwilling to play a backstage role, Waechter founded a new party, the *Mouvement Écologique Indépendent* (MEI), with little success afterward. Noël Mamère, former number two at GE, formed a new party, *Convergences Écologie Solidarité* (CES), that included defectors from the *Verts*. Other small ecological tickets also began to compete, notably *Alternative Rouge et Vert* (AREV), a collection of Communist renovators and militants from the former PSU.

The head of the *Verts*' new majority, Dominique Voynet, may be leading the party to a resurgence. Voynet comes from a family once active in the Socialist Party in the Jura region of France. The father had personal ties to the former leader of the PS's left-wing faction, Jean-Pierre Chevènement, whose local bastion is the Jura region. Born in 1957, Voynet was nevertheless a founding member of the *Verts* in 1984 and a veteran of the womens' and human rights movements as well. After becoming a spokesperson for the *Verts* in 1993, she was able to convince the party's activists to turn in a resolutely red/green direction in the next several years. An electoral pact with none other than the Socialist Party, signed in March of 1997, rewarded her efforts when President Jacques Chirac called early elections in June of that year. Riding popular sanctions to the government in favor of the Socialist-led opposition, the ecologists won seven seats in the National Assembly, hitherto barred to them (members of CES and AREV were among those elected). The new deputies included Cochet, Hascoët, and Mamère. Voynet herself gave up her seat to fill a new post, the Ministry for the Environment and Regional Policy. Though it is still early to tell, the *Verts*' fortunes, like those of the *Grünen*, may have reversed after the cleansing effect of a crisis.

Social and Political Background of the Green Electorate: Shifting Allegiances of the People of the Left

A look at the individuals who tend to vote for green parties in France and Germany reveals striking similarities. The average *Vert* or *Grüne* voter belongs to a group widely recognized as the most likely to support the new politics: middle-income, service sector professionals. Since the first green lists ran at the end of the 1970s, the profile of the average ecological voter has been fairly constant, regardless of the trends in which the parties' absolute numbers wax and wane.[23] In Germany, salaried service sector professionals represented 30 percent of those who voted for the ecologists in 1980, 26 percent in 1984, 35 percent in 1987, 35 percent in 1990.[24] In France, the figures run from 34 percent in 1978,[25] to 33.5 percent in 1984,[26] to 29 percent in 1989,[27] to 26 percent in 1993.[28] While enjoying comfortable salary levels, however, the average ecological voter was likely to place at the lower end of the middle-class scale and unlikely to hold an upper-management position.[29]

The ecological electorates in France and Germany were relatively young. In both cases however, there does seem to be a slight greying of the ecological voting bloc. The *Grüne* electorate between the age of eighteen and twenty-four went from 43.2 percent in 1980, to 23.2 percent in 1987, to 23 percent in 1990, whereas the twenty-five- to thirty-four-year-old bracket went from 27.2 percent in 1980, to 38.1 percent in 1987, to 40.8 percent in 1990.[30] This trend is evident in the data from France as well: in 1978, 27 percent were between eighteen and twenty-four, with 25 percent between twenty-five and thirty-four years; whereas in 1989 only 15 percent were between eighteen and twenty-five, with 31 percent between twenty-five and thirty-four.[31] The presence of students in higher education in the ranks of ecology party's supporters attests to this cohort's relative youth. In Germany, the number of students who had supported the *Grünen* was 49 percent in 1980, though the figure dropped to 20 percent in 1990.[32] Ecological voters generally have a high level of education. In France in 1989, 34 percent had degrees beyond high school.[33] Among *Grüne* voters, 45 percent had similar levels of education, vs. only 18 percent of the whole population. The ecologists generally have only marginal support from self-employed professionals or owners of businesses, or from manual workers. The *Grünen* made only slight gains with the latter group. In Germany, the proportion of workers went from 8 percent in 1980, to 13 percent in 1990,[34] whereas in France, the same group was stable 9.5 percent in 1978, to register again at 8 to 9 percent in 1993.[35]

Voters who support the ecology parties are most likely to choose an established party of the Left as an alternative. From one major election to another, about 30 to 50 percent of the ecologists' voters in either country defected from the main Center-Left party. In France, 44 percent of the voters for Antoine Waechter in the presidentials of 1988 voted for the Socialists in the parliamentary elections of March 1986. 39 percent of the voters who chose the *Verts* in the European Parliament elections of June 1989 voted for Mitterrand in the first turn of the presidentials of 1988. In the March 1993 Legislative elections, there was significant movement in the other direction.[36] About 17 percent of ecological voters (i.e., the combined scores of the *Verts* and *GE*) in the 1992 Regionals chose a leftist candidate (i.e., PS, PCF, or Extraparliamentary Left) in the first round of the 1993 Legislatives, and 45 percent of those who voted ecologist on the first round supported a PS candidate on the second.[37] The *Verts* also drew support from former voters of parties of the Extraparliamentary Left, and a small portion from Communist voters. In the Europeans of June 1989, the *Vert* list had the support of 22 percent of the votes for Alternative Left candidates in the presidentials of 1988 (i.e., those of Phillipe Boussel, Pierre Juquin, and Arlette Laguiller combined), and 8 percent of the Communists. Outside the left-leaning segment of the ecological vote, many others are either first-time voters, or supporters of the greens who abstain if no ecologist is present.[38] The remainder go to right-wing candidates: i.e., around 15 percent at most, and usually less than 10 percent.

In West Germany, respondents who supported the *Grünen* in an election to the *Bundestag* or *Landtag* had chosen the SPD in the previous election at the following rates: 36 percent in 1980, 20 percent in 1984, 28 percent in 1986, and 29 percent in 1990.[39] (The majority of others were first-time voters, plus a small portion who switched from the CDU/CSU or the FDP). Voters who picked the SPD on the first ballot chose the *Grünen* on the second in proportions similar to those we just noted; that is, 18 percent in 1980, 39.8 percent in 1983 and 31.2 percent in 1987. Conversely, among first ticket green voters, 28.6 percent chose the SPD for the second in 1980, 19.9 percent in 1983, and 20.3 percent in 1987.[40]

Whether or not they support the parties of the Left, the greens' electorate tend to support the ideals associated with it. Voters for the first green lists in France in the late 1970s were more moderate, but they moved Left later on.[41] A small but significant portion generally places on the far Left: 8.8 percent for the *Grünen*'s supporters, 12 percent for those of the *Verts*.[42] A plurality of green voters see themselves as center-left: 37.9 percent in Germany, and 43 percent in France. Thus, in each case, a majority fall on some left-of-center position. Of the rest, a significant portion see themselves as centrist: 38.3 percent of *Grüne* supporters and 28 percent of the *Verts*'s. That leaves 15 percent in Germany and 14 percent in France supporting the right and center-right combined. There is other evidence of support among *Grüne* and *Verts* voters for ideological positions traditionally associated with European socialism, for example, universal rights to economic advancement, for policy goals such as nationalizations, and support for trade union initiatives such as strikes and workplace democracy.[43]

Like the members of the *Grünen* and *Verts* themselves, the average green voter tends to be disenchanted with the mainstream parties of the Left. In France, 76 percent of ecological voters feel that the distinction between the parties of the Right and Left has little meaning, vs. 67 percent of all of the French.[44] 47 percent claim to have no confidence in their elected deputies, vs. 42 percent who do, a proportion found elsewhere only in the electorate of the National Front, France's far-right party.[45] In Germany, 27 percent of green supporters were "not satisfied with German democracy" in 1986, vs. 9 percent of the population; in 1990, the numbers were 17 percent vs. 9 percent, respectively.[46] Only 23 percent of *Grüne* voters claim to have any trust in the establishment parties, vs. 37 percent of the population; 26 percent express trust in the administrative sphere or parliament, vs. 48 percent for the whole population.[47]

Vert vs. *Grüne*: Structuring the Comparison

Though the French ecologists faced superior obstacles at the level of national politics, their social and political base was comparable to that of the *Grünen*. In addition, their transformation from radical movement/parties, through periods of crisis and fragmentation, and subsequent recomposition as potential partners in government, is similar. If we are interested in guaging the political viability of the ecologists' progammatic agenda, even France's closed institutional structure need not be viewed as an insurmountable obstacle to the greens there. The Federal Republic is relatively decentralized and geared toward minority representation, providing many opportunities for small parties like the Greens to make significant gains. Nevertheless since legislative and presidential elections in France follow a two-ballot system, smaller parties like the *Verts* can gain publicity and influence through successes in the first round.[48] Further, local, regional, and European elections in France follow proportional representation or a variant, and the French ecologists have won gains in these contests. The French regional councils gained more power and political significance as a result of the Decentralization Program of 1982, and ecologists now have seventy-five representatives sitting in the regional councils. Further, if we want to guage public interest in ecological politics in France vis-à-vis Germany, it is informative to compare votes rather than seats. With 14.5 percent in the 1992 regionals, French ecologists scored almost twice as high as the *Grünen*'s highest score in a national election. Even the 1993 parliamentary elections, a major contest with a majoritarian bias, where a green vote might be seen as a wasted one, the combined score of the main ecology parties alone was around 7 percent, close to the German Greens' highest parliamentary scores, and the ecological score reached the same level in the 1997 Legislative elections. Finally, although the French ecologists won no seats in the national parliament until 1997, they have exerted an impact on environmental policymaking in France. The electoral surge of the *Verts* spawned the creation of new agencies, financial resources, and political initiatives for the environment.[49]

To compare the two parties, therefore, we need only to select analytically similar periods in their history, taking into account the fact that, in chronological terms, the French ecologists made their niche in their party system a little later. Further, due to their clear electoral and political links with the ecologists, the status of the socialist parties should be a key factor explaining the variations in the ecological strategies. We need to inquire further why social movements like ecology and feminism have always had to face Left once they choose the parliamentary route in the first place, what might be the new entrants' sources of strategic advantages and disadvantages, and the problems that arise when two progressive parties compete for a similar electorate. For that purpose, we turn to theoretical works that analyze social movements and party systems.

Chapter *Three*

Theoretical Considerations: Ideology and Strategy in Contemporary Party Competition

The Political Context: Social Movements and Parties of Protest

Social movements that predated and prefigured the rise of the greens in Europe spoke in many tongues, but had one greater message. The organs of democratic governance were faltering, and popular movements were prepared to take politics into their own hands. By the end of the 1970s, oil shocks and flagging economic performance had undermined postwar growth and the consensus surrounding its equitable distribution. One of the pillars of this consensus, organized labor, began to withdraw its support, and portions turned toward militancy and demands for worker's control over production. Advocates of the rights of women confronted political representatives, once oblivious, with a novel challenge. Citizens' action groups formed to protest the failures of nuclear and military technocrats to guarantee their security and even their survival. By organizing political parties to represent these movements, the greens aimed to carry their transformative motifs and spontaneous modes of action to the heart of the political arena, and thus to transform it.

Influential works on social movements and on parties that apppeared during this period of social and political unrest addressed the problem from very different perspectives. Conservative writers claimed that the West faced a "crisis of governability," in which popular expectations exceeded the ability of democratic governments to respond.[1] Since the representative institutions of the democratic state guaranteed that this surplus of popular demands were all legitimate, these writers proposed to limit the representative function itself. Party systems theory fell into this category.[2] Its adherents were concerned with the capacity of parties and parliaments to channel or limit the most intense popular demands and create stable government. Party systems theorists took little note of the social and historical origins of these demands. They concentrated on how the strategic interaction between parties or formal electoral institutions may shape them.[3]

Post-Marxist or radical authors agreed that political systems were strained by new and increased demands, and warned that a "systems overload" or "legitimation crisis" might be the result.[4] Yet these authors were more concerned with interpreting and, by the same token, with advocating the new demands. Writers specifically interested in the new social movements fall in this category (we refer to these as NSM theorists). In contrast to the formalism and state-centrism of party systems theory, NSM theory is historical and society centered. Whereas conservatives wanted to limit the demands made on the state and parliamentary system, NSM theorists asked how to heighten their intensity.

Despite the latent antagonism, there are points of contact between the two perspectives. One underlying premise links them: ideas have weight in politics. In addition, they concur that it is strategic for new entrants in the political system to develop a comprehensive ideology and stress the radical distinctiveness of their ideas. Furthermore, both acknowledge that participating in formal political institutions can eventually transform and perhaps weaken these ideas—and with that, the movements' mission. The two sets of literature diverge on whether or not engaging in parliamentary competition or undergoing this process of transformation is desirable.

There is, in fact, no need to see the aims of movement and party as mutually exclusive. Nor does the choice to participate in elections imply a single fate for movement-based parties. The ideologies of progressive parties can, at times, address both the demands of supporting social movements and appeal to a wider circle of interested citizens or voters. In other words, they may speak to both identity and efficacy. Our aim here is to explain when and how they move in one direction or another, and to understand how the two imperatives can conflict. As we have stressed, competition and interaction between progressive organizations, such as ecologists and socialists, heightens the tensions between identity and efficacy. We shall refer to a third set of literature that deals with the strategic choices of socialist parties and trade unions to develop the concepts of identity and efficacy, and to model the iterated games between the two competing organizations. That will allow us to suggest why one strategy or another is rational in each situation, and to highlight the limits of each strategy.

Parties and Party Systems: Organizational Interests and Ideological Competition

Michels set the intellectual agenda for both party systems and social movement theorists. In Michels' view, the decision to enter parliamentary participation was ultimately counterproductive to the aims of radical social movements. Class conflict required organization, and that process in turn would distort the goals and demands that had led the working class to organize in the first place. It ought to come as no surprise, then, that strategy was not an explicit problem in Michels's work. Once the game of participation was chosen, the game was over for the party or union leaders as much as it was for the class they were supposed to represent. Further, ideology played no role in the process. Michels believed that comprehensive and independent ideologies would become irrelevant over time, since organization and leadership meant compromise with conservative political forces and accommodation to their views.[5]

Contemporary literature on parties and party systems, despite a huge debt to Michels, does not necessarily share his view that the competitive process proceeds in a single direction toward oligarchy and political compromise. The contemporary theorists believed that the process of competition could intensify ideology as well as diminish it. They tended to argue that parties needed ideology to attract uncertain voters and to distinguish themselves from other parties. In certain situations, that could induce ideological polarlization rather than convergence. For example, whereas Michels saw only incrementalism and ideological convergence, Duverger saw polarization and differentiation, or "dualism" as he called it. "Every policy," Duverger argued, "implies a choice between two kinds of solution . . . synthesis is a power only of mind. Action involves choice and politics involves action."[6] In Duverger's view, popular opinion and elite policy choices were governed by this dualistic tendency.

Downs's concept of party competition was, like Duverger's, defined by a clear opposition between the ideologies of the Left and Right, and by their characteristic policies of government intervention and market freedom, respectively. In Downs's framework, parties shift their programs tactically along this Left/Right scale, or "space," whether to move closer to a winning position or to distance themselves from issues for which they have little credibility or support. Where they cannot be sure of parties' actions on a certain issue, voters gain clues from this ideological positioning.[7] Downs believed that party ideologies would generally converge in the long run, and thus gave us the well-known "Downsian effect." Yet he did forsee situations in which the opposite could occur, and even in two-party systems, which he and Duverger thought were more stable than multiparty systems.[8] If a major party moves in a certain direction to try to capture a majority, alienated voters might defect to other parties with the sole aim of forcing it back toward their views in the next elections. Similarly, when an established party compromises its original goals in the quest to form majorities, "extremists" within it may form new parties to force the main organization back to its original position. "In situations like this," Downs asserts, "it is a movement of party ideology, not of voter distribution, which gives rise to a new party." Further, "this type of new party will appear almost exclusively in two-party systems. Fear of these blackmail parties may counteract the centripetal pull normal to such systems."[9]

Downs is saying that new, radical parties emerge as the result of opportunities created by the normal operation of the democratic process, and not on the basis of social grievances alone. If we see the greens as such a party, that would explain why they often strongly resist moves toward alliance and ideological rapprochement with the parties of the mainstream Left. If the greens formed parties in the first place to oppose the ideological convergence between the parties of the Right and Left (hence the slogan that they are "neither Right nor Left"), they could be expected to view any move toward negotiation with either one as simply one more bulwark for two-party dominance.

Sartori's work moves still further from Michels than Duverger's or Downs's. He accords considerable power to ideology and the types of parties that advance it. Like Duverger and Downs, Sartori believed that multiparty systems tend toward ideological polarization and instability, but he added a new variable to the number of parties involved.[10] The presence of "antisystem parties" was the decisive factor, and it led to what Sartori identified as "polarized pluralism," wherein the overall direction of ideological competition flowed toward each extreme. Antisystem parties are parties that seek to overthrow the system (some of them, of course, such as West European communist parties, wind up operating peaceably in the same system for long periods of time). They are "ideological," in the pejorative sense; their stated goals are not feasible. Further, they threaten the stability of their system through the "politics of outbidding." That is, they continuously escalate their promises to the electorate to outflank more moderate parties, forcing these other parties to move in a similar direction, in turn leading to an "inflation of expectations"—and social unrest or political paralysis may result. Like Downs, Sartori implicitly recognizes that the demands of competition themselves, and not just the self-interests of leaders, give protest parties an incentive to intensify their demands and sharpen their ideological differences with respect to their competitors (though Sartori clearly deplores the effects that may have on the whole system). In sum, party systems theorists would agree that parties at the extreme ends of multiparty systems have a special interest in defining and differentiating their ideas sharply with respect to their closest competitor.[11]

We know, then, that new parties need ideology. Yet we still do not know why more ideological parties, such as the greens, develop varying ideologies. Party systems theory, in which ideology appears to play such a central role, cannot explain the content of a given ideology, which is viewed as originating from endogenous social factors. Parties maneuver within a predetermined space. They may adjust their programs tactically, but the ideological substance is still virtually the same. Parties simply emphasize ideology in different degrees. Left and Right, of course, have different ideologies. But one half is essentially the mirror image of that of the other; that is, both are divided into extreme and moderate tendencies. The possibility that each might have a distinct dynamic is not discussed.

Since party systems theory concentrates on system-level outcomes such as stability or polarization (or else on systemwide effects such as those of ballot mechanisms on seat apportionment), it cannot say anything meaningful about any individual party within the system. The question is the fate of the whole system, not the parts. Considered from this vantage point, green parties threaten to burst the analytical terms of party systems theory. Are they antisystem or prosystem parties? Do they seek to undermine the very foundations on which the competitive system rests (i.e., material growth)? Or do they seek to restore a healthy measure of democratic choice to an ossified party establishment (i.e., by opposing the convergence between Right and Left)? Are they the enemies of democracy or its tribunes?

As in the case of any systems theory, we cannot explain the parts (parties or their strategies) with reference to the whole (the party system). This should be especially true for antisystem parties: since their aim is to change the system, they cannot be fully understood within the terms of its formal mechanics. While paying attention to the real constraints that competition imposes on parties, we should bracket away questions about the functioning or malfunctioning of the whole party system and concentrate on the portions of it that most directly and immediately affect the greens. That is, we should focus on the Left half of the party system, on the spectrum of progressive organizations competing to lead reform of the system. And as party systems theory does suggest, we should focus on the greens' main competitors, established parties of the Center-Left.

We do not need to view the greens' actions as irresponsible or desperate moves to outbid an adversary otherwise poised to take the reins of power. What they do is probe and exploit the very real contradictions in their competitors' handling of government and of

their own supporters' demands. The challengers may make proposals that are not just quantitatively different (e.g., higher
wages) but qualitatively different (e.g., the need to address other
themes besides wages). The next set of literature addresses these
qualitative reforms the ecologists seek and the dynamics of green/
left relations. That allows us to understand what binds the new
social movements to the "old" ones (working-class or socialist
movements) and the parties that represent them, and what sets
them apart.

Political Economy: Green Parties and the Contradictions of Social Democracy

One approach to ecology and the new social movements, which we
may call a "political economic approach," sees them as a symptom
of strains in corporatist industrial relations and in the political
coalition supporting social democracy. Corporatism refers to a
form of industrial management in which working-class organizations have an official status; corporatist arrangements tend to appear in tandem with a large welfare state and powerful social
democratic parties. Once a pillar of the postwar social and political compromise in Europe, corporatism came under increasing
criticism as that compromise began to unravel.[12] In the political
economic approach, latent antagonisms between an established
Left, headed by working-class and party leaders, and a New Left,
composed of progressive sectors of labor or students and intellectuals, lead to a political and ideological schism. Ecology and allied
movements, in this view, are a renegade part of the Left, aiming
toward a new push for reform.[13]

Opposition to corporatist arrangements is spearheaded by
workers in rising industrial sectors, who work with new technology rather than in heavy industry, and their allies in the independent Left. They demand more control over production processes,
regulation of the workplace environment and limits on harmful
products.[14] Conservative working-class leaders, their supporters
in the manual working class in more traditional sectors, and their
allies at the top of the party hierarchy tend to reject these reforms
as too extensive and destabilizing. At the same time, global economic contraction and a newly assertive managing class put

working-class leaders on the defensive. The strain becomes still
more intense in a situation where a social democratic party leads
or participates in the government. In that case, the party is con-
strained to manage the problems of a complex, interdependent
capitalist economy while still trying to respond to the heightened
expectations for reform it may instill in their working-class and
progressive constituents. As conflicts reach a pitch, the independent Left may break away from the socialist political coalition to
form new parties that reject the idea that class conflict or class-
based demands should be a privileged or central category for
progressive politics. Kitschelt has applied this analysis to cross-
national empirical tests in order to discern the relationship between corporatism and the presence of significant New Left or
ecology parties.[15] Sampling countries that have high welfare state
expenditures, low strike activity, and significant tenure in power
of left-wing governments, all associated with the presence of corporatism, he finds a positive association between these factors
and the emergence of ecology parties.

The political economic approach may suggest why the new
movements break away from the established parties of the Left. It
says less, however, about why or how they regroup in the form of
ecology parties. As we noted in the last chapter, the New Left was
important in the reaction to social democracy. But it never mounted
an effective electoral challenge to it. The new movements disaffected with what they saw as the narrow class focus of the established Left rallied behind the green symbolism of ecology parties,
not behind the democratic socialist or *autogestionnaire* demands of
independent Left parties like the PSU in France, which foundered
while the ecologists gained. If discrete environmental demands
were present in the New Left agenda, that does not fully explain
the emergence and impact of comprehensive ecological ideologies in
the parties formed by some of the same activists later on.

Further, the internal rebellion incited by a left-wing party's
participation in government may be broader, in terms of the range
of disaffected groups and thus in impact, than a struggle within
the trade unions alone. It is the party that controls the government, not the trade union movement, and it is the party that suffers the most direct consequences of holding office. This is why
electoral socialist parties like the *Parti Socialiste*, otherwise un-
burdened by union/party links, and at times quite effective at ral-

lying New Left support, nevertheless suffered severe sanctions at the polls only when its tenure in power reached ten years. All governing parties, including leftist parties, corporatist or not, place a value on economic growth, and environmentalists can and will challenge them for that, as was the case in France. Further, socialist parties in government, even "modern" or New Left-oriented socialist parties like the PS, tend to marginalize or deflect potentially divisive programmatic themes such as feminism or ecology.[16] Conflicts over these questions have erupted between radical youth movement activists and party elites—both middle class—as much as within the working-class structure itself. Even if it is granted that unrest and rebellion in the socialist coalition provide opportunities for a political challenge to erupt, we still do not know what ensures its success. If contemporary social movements form with new goals, what means—or strategies—do they use to advance them?

Resource Mobilization: Organizing Social Movements

A second approach to contemporary social movements sees their capacity to organize as a key resource and a prerequisite to their ability to formulate any strategy for social change. Proponents of the resource mobilization school argue that social movements are not vehicles for the inchoate rebellion of alienated out-groups, but are a form of rational resource management.[17] Resource mobilization theorists thus do not focus on the nature of peoples' grievances, which they assume are present at all times in all societies. The emphasis is on their capacity to organize to redress those grievances. McCarthy and Zald took note of some key elements of organizational strength in modern social movements: alliances with groups with different demands or grievances, their ability to instill awareness of grievances in the populace, and the level of support they received from interlocking social movement networks.[18] Money, labor, and information were all requirements for effective organization. According to Piven and Cloward, since sheer disruption brings publicity, even the poorest and most alienated groups were capable of what was, in effect, a rational use of protest as a means to an end.[19]

Parties, in this perspective, may be an effective means for mobilizing protest, although McCarthy and Zald do not say so explicitly. If social movements require "minimal organizational
resources," even loosely structured parties like green parties can
provide them. Unlike many social movement organizations, they
are permanent, receive nationwide publicity, attract a variety of
supporters, and bring in funds in the form of public campaign fi-
nancing. Because of their promise for more permanent agitation
and challenges to the establishment, parties of protest can move
individuals and groups outside the central social movement to
join the cause. Modern social movements must "transform mass
and elite publics into sympathizers." Similarly, new parties steal
leading parties' votes, ensuring that the latter discover a personal sympathy for the issues that attract those lost votes. The
benefits flow in both directions between protest movements and
protest parties. If there is a network of social movement organizations to parallel party activities, the former can test new leaders, spread word of new issues, and provide ready-made support
in campaigns.[20]

In light of this symbiosis between party and movement, it is
puzzling that many resource mobilization theorists see the formation of parties out of grassroots social movements as a form of
stagnation and loss of momentum. Tilly notes that there is necessarily a "break in the life history of any group that passes between
challenger and member."[21] In his study of the Italian New Left organization, *Lotta Continua*, Tarrow holds that its decision to form
into a party seeking votes was an act of desperation, taken at a
point where it could no longer mobilize students and workers by
any other means.[22] Piven and Cloward argue that after long periods of successful mobilization, movements suffered setbacks when
their leaders begin to channel disruption and elites coopt their demands.[23] Kitschelt and Offe, not practitioners of the resource mobilization approach, have viewed the evolution of new social
movements into parties more positively. They argue that these
parties are more successful with, or at any rate innocuous without, alliances with the leading parties, particularly left-wing
ones.[24] Still, their perspective represents the opposite side of the
same Michelsian coin that resource mobilization writers trade in.
Whatever their evaluation of the situation, party formation is
viewed as a unidirectional movement toward accommodation to

existing structures, and a corollary is that the most radical demands will (or should) therefore become muted.

Recalling the insights of the party systems theorists, we submit that it may be rational, in some situations, for newly formed parties to faithfully transmit the most radical demands of protest movements and to remain in but not of the political system. As Downs's account of the origins of protest parties might suggest, the alternative of moderation and compromise is equally fraught with tension.

The resource mobilization school, like the party systems theorists, avoids discussion of the content and specificity of political demands in order to focus on the formal dynamics of certain types of organizations. It follows that the resource mobilization approach tends to see new social movements as one instance in a larger continuum of all social movement activity. But the demands of the new social movements, and the parties that arise from them, often center on the identities of their protagonists, and that may set them apart from other social movements. What they use to get what they want is intimately connected with who they are. To grasp the specificity of identity politics, we need to explore when and why it arose, and examine its characteristic demands more closely.

New Social Movements: Expression over Power?

Unlike all the previous approaches, NSM theory focuses on ideas and actions of the new movements, viewing them as radically distinct from other forms of politics, including class-based social movements. Parallel to this shift in concerns is a shift in approach. The previous theoretical approaches were structuralist or realist. The analyses centered on underlying economic interests or on organized struggles for power, or both. In contrast, the NSM approach enters an interpretive mode. NSM theorists try to convey the distinctive qualities and common objectives of what is actually an extremely heterogenous set of movements and issues. It may interpret them as manifestations of deep structural changes in contemporary societies that are making the transition from industrial to postindustrial paradigms. It may identify as sites for opposition the commodification of personal life generated by marketing and media, the apparently benign institutions that actually serve as agencies for social control, such as the welfare state or information systems, or the cultural domination inherent in patriarchial or Western imperial societies. In this view, new social movements are struggling not only over specific goods but over the fundamental assumptions about who shall be involved, or who has the right to make claims about goods—hence the term *identity politics*. NSM theory often attempts to enter into the consciousness of those who bear these identities, and thus sometimes seem, like those they study, to privilege self-expression over instrumental action.[25]

It is an open question, then, whether new social movements, or the theorists writing about them, believe that strategy—in the sense of gaining a decisive advantage over an adversary—is feasible or desirable. The focus is on changing the ways we think about politics, not engaging in organized politics itself. Habermas's influential concept of communicative action conveys what is at stake in this goal of relative detachment from power and instrumentality. To engage in communicative action is to determine fundamental values according to which social action itself takes place, in a context utterly free from unequal control over information or over moral standards. Habermas opposes this concept to that of strategic action, which implies gaining advantage over an adversary.[26]

In practice, the boundaries between communicative action and strategic action are not as clear. Habermas, who makes the distinction between the two strictly for the sake of analysis, acknowledges this. Touraine, for another example, has argued that as social life becomes more secularized, and organized around the control of information, its cultural foundations themselves become open to struggle and strategic action among contending groups. If movements or parties can question or subvert tacit assumptions of political discourse or contest unfair interpretations, they thereby shift the game of politics to their advantage. If they can define new issues that should be the subject of politics, they become, at the same time, the legitimate representatives of those issues.[27]

It may be strategic, for example, for spontaneous movements with narrow grievances to elevate their demands or agendas from a specific to a more general level—that is, to transform ideas into ideologies. A particular movement has to offer some view of social

change that can attract outsiders and oppose prevailing defini-
tions of order with a coherent alternative; it cannot be effective by
denouncing the existing order alone. The more effectively they
can explain how the changes they seek serve a more general notion of rationality, the more effective they are. Touraine refers to
the workers' movement at the turn of the century as an example:
workers' representatives not only sought to establish workers'
control within the factory, but argued that that could reduce inef-
ficiency and waste.[28] In this same vein, social movements have to
take the offensive in the domain of ideology. It is not enough just
to identify an adversary. Its character or actions have to be reeval-
uated and represented as an instance or cause of a more fundamental source of social problems, or as a contradiction of some
shared or stated values. Touraine argues that this is what distin-
guishes a social movement from a pressure group.[29] Habermas
likewise holds that the only truly offensive movements are those
that can appeal to some universal value, one that is claimed by a
dominant group as a source of its own legitimacy but contradicted
by its actions or its exclusive prerogatives.[30]

Finally, many NSM theorists acknowledge that the new movements cannot remain totally opposed to parliamentary and public
institutions.[31] Cohen and Arato argue that, due to the heterogeneity of the identities different movements address, they have
an interest in supporting institutions that possess at least the potential for fairness and open public debate.[32] Further, they suggest that a need for concerted action, on several fronts, implies a
deliberate, long-range strategy. That in turn implies the need for
a permanent organization to enact it: that is, a political party.

We have arrived deductively at a conclusion the ecologists and
other new social movements reached in practice. Sheer spontane-
ity and independence risked permanent marginality, and participation in formal institutions may have been the lesser evil.[33] In
contrast to the claims of resource mobilization theorists, party formation might be the logical route for social movements to follow in
order to fuse their essential themes and engage in more concerted
forms of strategic action. The contribution of NSM theory to our
understanding of party competition is to introduce the element of
communicative action—a dialogue about the fundamentals on
which action rests—into the strategic repertoire parties may
employ. Party systems theory holds that parties can effectively

represent interests only if there is basic consensus on the rules of competition. NSM theory suggests that the rules of the game themselves can and should be the subject of political action and struggle.[34] Party systems theory sees ideology as disjoined from reality. In contrast, NSM theory sees it as a creative and positive force, actually constituting political and social reality. For party systems theorists, parties with the most coherent and consistent ideologies are also the most radical, and the least likely to be responsible to the system; ideology, in this sense, is the enemy of democracy. In the NSM perspective, the more ideological parties draw on the most fundamental principles of democracy, restoring it in periods of decline.

NSM theory, then, tells us that new movements may have certain advantages in reshaping the political debate or redeploying accepted principles to their own advantage. Since their work is speculative and interpretive in nature, however, NSM theorists usually do not discuss specific strategies for actual movements or parties. If we want to know why a certain party would choose one type of strategy or another out of the range of options NSM theory outlines, we need to examine the tradeoffs each choice implies, and what types of political opportunities and constraints they might respond to.

Strategic Choices:
Between Movement and Party

A final set of literature examines the compromises and tradeoffs of the industrial workers' movements and the socialist parties often allied with them as they turned toward institutionalized politics to realize their demands. Offe and Wiesenthal focus on the internal politics of trade unions. In their analysis, workers' interests are not merely economic. The quality of their lives is at stake. Workers' organizations address not only higher wages but a varied and nonnegotiable set of life-chances or physical needs.[35] To reach consensus on these diverse needs, members of working-class organizations have to be allowed to engage in an open process of communication and deliberation within their organizations. Yet this communicative rationality, centered on fundamental human needs and the dialogue that can articulate it, comes into conflict with the rationality of concerted political action and organization. Echoing Michels, Offe and Wiesenthal argue that workers' interests have to be defined in terms appropriate for negotiation, compromise, and organizational continuity and predictability.[36] Union leaders or organizers have an interest in this process of redefinition, since they seek official recognition and financial resources. That in turn devalues the more vital and comprehensive interests of individual workers and diminishes the possibility of democratic internal debate. As the organization benefits its leaders at the expense of its working-class constituents, the latter turn toward their own strategy of mobilization and militancy. Hence Offe and Wiesenthal (departing in this case from Michels) envision a cyclic pattern between extremes of movement-based contention and institutional predictability.

Przeworski's work examines the process of mobilizing workers in the electoral arena. Przeworski's central problem is identity formation—that is, the formation of class identity in the consciousness of individual workers. Socialist parties are the driving force in forming class identity. They organize workers for the purpose of major political reform, instilling awareness of the common (i.e., class) interest in these reforms (i.e., socialism). Socialist parties *qua* parties also address other constituencies, however. They need to form class alliances to get elected and effect the desired reforms. Thus, socialist parties address interests either partially opposed to or at any rate different from those of workers. That in turn undermines the original bases for mobilizing workers to the party in the first place: "class identity ceases to be the only conceivable source of workers' commitments."[37]

We shall identify the underlying problem in these analyses of collective action as a tradeoff between identity and efficacy.[38] Political organizations promoting social change face two imperatives: ensuring genuine movement toward change and organizing political alliances to effect it. The guarantee that the organization will press intense, often nonnegotiable demands for change conflicts with the guarantee of diversity (in Przeworski's framework) or of the continuity of the organization itself (in that of Offe and Wiesenthal). A strategy of efficacy means articulating the demands of a range of social movements. By expanding the scope of issues addressed, the aim is to rallying the broadest possible base of supporters. The process of contesting elections responds to this arithmetic imperative: support is measured in votes, not in intensity of individual commitment. The party appeals to any activists or voters marginally interested in new social movements or their issues (such as the environment, for example, in the case of green parties) no matter how narrowly those issues are defined. That move is clearly rational: if successful, it encroaches on the leading parties' votes, and they in turn must address the new party's issues. Further, the new party's leaders receive a strong mandate to act on these issues as participants in government.

A strategy of identity means that the party stresses the characteristic demands of a single social movement. Borrowing the term *identity* from the NSM literature, we use it to denote the communicative strategy that literature advanced: that is, an emphasis on models comprehensive and fundamental change capable of undermining an established normative consensus. Identity also addresses a strategic imperative posited by party systems theorists: it defines the party as something wholly apart from the others, and the sole authentic representative of the movement's characteristic demands. An identity strategy is also rational from an internal point of view. It secures the loyalty of militants, activists from allied movements, and the most reliable voters willing to carry out the party's activities and thus to guarantee its survival. Identity often implies deferring actual movement—that is, obtaining tangible gains—in the name of guaranteeing the authenticity and purity of the mobilizing ideals of the supporting social movement.

Sacrificing efficacy for identity has its costs. Electoral support may be deep (that is, reliable), but not wide (that is, extensive in numbers). To maintain credibility with its base, the party has to keep up the intensity and momentum of demands for change. That in turn risks alienating its more moderate or marginal supporters who favor incremental reforms. Since its agenda tends to privilege certain issues or themes over others, the party becomes defined by them. It thus sacrifices its credibility when it moves to embrace other issues. Finally, insofar as the radical communicative strategy can succeed in the short term, it leads to a paradox in the longer term. It acts within the parliamentary system, convincing more and more people of the bankruptcy of that very system, and thus contradicts its fundamental claim that the system is incapable of positive change.[39]

Sacrificing identity for efficacy also has costs. The party must expand its range of programmatic themes to satisfy as many interested groups as possible. Broadening the agenda comes at the expense of clear commitment to any single cause. In the process, it may blur its program, sacrificing coherent formulations for vague rallying symbols and ideals.Thus it risks losing the party's most intense and interested supporters (for example, the working class, in Przeworski's formulation). Programmatic vagueness itself can make incrementalism and coalition bargaining more attractive.[40] Without clear ideal premiums for individual or group mobilization, there is a need to achieve immediate results in order to secure activists' or supporting movements' commitment at all. That in turn partly legitimizes the coalition partners in other parties as potential representatives of the new issues, diminishes the need for a new party, and creates a loss of momentum behind broader change.

With this understanding of the strategic choices progressive parties make, we can now model some of the situations in which they interact and compete. Competition with other parties narrows the strategic options for any single party (especially in the case of smaller newcomers like the greens), and the process of competition will intensify the tensions each strategy entails. We use the generic terms *socialist* and *green* (or *ecology*), by the way, to refer to the real parties from which we derive the model. But the formal dynamic itself should hold for any two progressive parties that compete. Tables 3.1 through 3.4 present possible combinations of strategies and the political implications for each party that may result.

In theory, there may be situations of equilibrium, in which two parties coexist and each one has stable electoral scores. Imagine a socialist party that maximizes efficacy without addressing identity. It would be a catch-all party: a large organization with a centrist profile that reliably draws a wide range of voters on the basis of vague, consensual issues. This would hardly be a progressive or left-wing party at all, since it would not have, nor have need for, any constituency intensely mobilized for reform. In this situation, a green party could conceivably coexist in a state of equilibrium with the socialist party (see table 3.1). With the socialist party maximizing efficacy, the green party would place strict emphasis on identity. The latter would be, in effect, a single-issue party. It

Table 3.1   Static Model

SOCIALIST STRATEGY: STRONG EFFICACY, LOW IDENTITY	ECOLOGIST STRATEGY: LOW EFFICACY, STRONG IDENTITY
Alliances not necessary	Alliances not feasible
Programmatic accord not necessary	Programmatic accord not possible
Reliable, diverse electorate	Reliable, highly circumscribed electorate

would have an extremely circumscribed base of loyal sympathizers who are not likely to defect to the socialists. Alliances between the two would not be feasible for either constituency, especially the ecologists, since their views and issues would be mutually exclusive.[41] This situation would be static, since there would be no real competition between the two parties and no strategic interaction.

A socialist party, of course, may emphasize identity and sacrifice efficacy. It would then resemble a typical West European Communist Party. It would mobilize a definite and intensely alienated constituency (members of the working class) around a program of significant social change, and would tend to reject compromise with parties that represent the status quo. There could be a state of equilibrium here, too, if all else were equal (see table 3.2). The two organizations would address distinct constituencies with distinct thematic profiles. They would attract only a small portion of the total electorate due to the minority status of these parties' constituencies. This model actually has a direct practical application: green parties and communist parties do tend to target distinct social bases, and rarely confront one another as real adversaries.[42]

In practice, there are no pure strategies of identity and efficacy. As we have stressed, real parties have to try to straddle the two imperatives. Further, there are no actual party systems where the green/socialist or green/communist standoffs in tables 3.1 and 3.2 would not be complicated by the presence of another competitor of the Left, Center-Left, or Center (and the last two may compete

Table 3.2 Static Model

SOCIALIST STRATEGY: LOW EFFICACY, STRONG IDENTITY	ECOLOGIST STRATEGY: LOW EFFICACY, STRONG IDENTITY
Alliances not feasible	Alliances not feasible
Programmatic accord not possible	Programmatic accord not possible
Reliable, highly circumscribed electorate	Reliable, highly circumscribed electorate

with the greens for votes). Nor are there any systems, of course, without a right-wing opposition that would be only too content to look on an ecology party and a left-wing party each reliably winning a small portion of the vote and refusing to join in any strategic offensive, as in table 3.2. Therefore the situations of equilibria outlined in tables 3.1 and 3.2 would not hold. Each party will be trying to arrive at the best strategy for the situation, while trying to finesse the tensions it entails—and all that while trying to respond to its competitor's moves. Modelling all of the possible combinations of parties and strategies involved, however, would yield far more combinations than we could handle. For the sake of parsimony, we designate the strategy of the leading socialist party as the most immediate constraint on the greens' strategy, while acknowledging that other parties to its Left or Right do in turn pull the socialist party in one direction or another. We have chosen empirical cases where the socialist strategies point in clearly contrasting directions, one pulled toward the Right of its party system, the other, to the Left.

In the next two situations, the iterations of competitive games between greens and socialists come into play. Table 3.3 outlines a situation where the socialist party combines identity and efficacy.[43] With broad yet intense support, the socialist party is both powerful and strongly committed to reform (Phase 1). It represents a range of progressive movements, while also commanding a portion of the center. Thus the ecology party's potential efficacy is limited. The most rational strategy for the ecologists is to stress identity over efficacy all the more intensely (Phase 2). The ecology

Table 3.3 Dynamic Model

	SOCIALIST STRATEGY: STRONG IDENTITY, STRONG EFFICACY	ECOLOGIST STRATEGY: STRONG IDENTITY, LOW EFFICACY
Phase 1	Powerful. Mandate for major reform in government with the support of diverse progressive movements and voters.	Weak. Available support limited. Strategy difficult to develop. Rational strategy is to embrace any movement identity outside socialist coalition.
Phase 2	Tension between movement constituencies, sanctions for holding power, factional conflict.	Begins to draw full available support for distinct identity. Insulated from problems in socialist coalition.
Phase 3	Party attempts to recapture lost support by embracing new identities (including that of ecologists). Movements reject party's compromise and defect from coalition.	Success reinforces identity. Socialist defectors rally to ecology party. Rejection of any alliance offers and new programmatic material.
Phase 4	Major political sanctions. Loss of power.	Rigid adherence to identity. Political isolation, dogmatism, low credibility on new issues.

party must address some identity marginalized by the socialists' supporting coalition, and stress its ideological and political independence from its competitor. When this succeeds, the socialist party, already experiencing the tensions of combining the two, will try to coopt the greens' identity (Phase 3). The latter will reject that overture—and that is rational because it has staked its identity on its distance from the socialist party. Still, in Phase 4, the socialist party itself reaches a critical stage, and loses a significant share of votes and, presumably, of government power. Ironically, that creates opportunities for the ecologists to coopt defectors, and thus address efficacy. But only a major crisis in the green party's support is sufficient to change the party leadership and overcome the rigidities in its strategy (that is the case for either type of party in any situation). This situation is modelled on the dynamics of green/socialist competition in France.

In the last situation we discuss, the socialist party has a weak identity and poor efficacy (see table 3.4). It suffers strong political sanctions, and the green party thus has the opportunity to address a range of identities alienated by the socialists (Phase 1).

The result is that the greens combine identity and efficacy: they embrace a wide range of support while maintaining a progressive profile. Note, however, that this success is less the result of any coherent strategy at all than of a political windfall. The greens' identity is formed negatively, the result of the socialists'

Table 3.4   Dynamic Model

	SOCIALIST STRATEGY: WEAK IDENTITY, LOW EFFICACY	ECOLOGIST STRATEGY: STRONG IDENTITY, STRONG EFFICACY
Phase 1	Politically weak. Alienates core supporting groups and marginal voters.	Strong mandate for change. Support of range of movements with distinct identities. Little need for clear strategy.
Phase 2	Electoral sanctions and significant decline in power, loss of government control.	Many opportunities to share power. Tension between competing movement constituencies.
Phase 3	Sanctions persist. Leadership crisis.	Internal conflicts weaken the party's identity. Sanctions weaken its efficacy.
Phase 4	Strategic shift possible as new leaders begin to embrace movement identities alienated by old leaders and competitor's themes.	Internal crisis. Major loss of support. Leadership turnover.

default in representing progressive movements. Furthermore, competing identities exist within in the diverse green coalition, and the tensions come to the fore (Phase 2). At that point, increasing opportunities to share power, the result of the greens' very success, heighten the latent conflict between factions inside the party. The conflicts then begin to strain supporters' ability to identify with the green party as its overall position becomes unclear (Phase 3). Meanwhile, the socialist party has reached the point of crisis, as its support diminishes past acceptable levels. The crisis finally allows a leadership change, and the socialist party now has the flexibility to coopt the greens' themes. Thus the socialists can encroach on the greens' identity, and the latter experience the full results of the tensions of combining identity and efficacy (Phase 4). This situation corresponds to the dynamics of green/socialist competition in Germany.

In any single election we shall examine, a viable strategy for the ecology party in question should combine the imperatives of identity and efficacy as fully as possible. There are two operational variables. First, the new parties must construct a *defining identity*: they are forced to define who they are in terms of who they are not. That means their programmatic documents or leadership discourse should specify the themes or attitudes that separate the ecologists from the prevailing counterparty. The greens should also have an *alternative program* that outlines concrete reforms, whether aimed toward environmental protection or other issues (exactly which depends on the ways these are defined or evaluated in their overall identity). The reforms need not be feasible in the short term. We assume that rational voters reward the ecologists for showing what direction they would take if they were granted even a small portion of the power needed to achieve the proposals.

Up to this point, we have looked at green parties as units and assumed that they act more or less in concert on the basis of one strategy or another. That does some injustice to the political and ideological diversity of the leaders and activists within green parties. A variety of perspectives as to what each party's identity ought to be coexisted, sometimes uneasily, inside these organizations. In the next chapter, we look inside the parties to understand how internal currents in each one viewed the party's overall political situation, and inquire further into why one or another might eventually prevail and shape the identity of the whole organization.

Chapter *Four*

Ideology and Competition Inside Ecology Parties: Reexamining Herbert Kitschelt's "Logics of Party Formation"

Introduction

One of the most striking aspects of ecology parties has been the level of conflict within them. Their radically democratic format has required that no particular perspective could be suppressed by a party elite. The intensity of individuals' commitments to their particular cause meant that common ground was sometimes hard to reach. Conflict has turned on the very ends the party sought: did the greens really stand for environmental safety and health, or social justice, institutional reforms, cultural tolerance, or sustainable global development? Conflicts were sometimes more strictly political: what course of action would advance these ends? Ideological debates have often become entangled with leadership contests, leading to debilitating public feuds. The challenge for social scientists, as much as for the ecologists themselves, is to transcend this embarrassment of ideological riches and determine which perspectives might be the most politically viable, or strategic, and in which contexts.

Herbert Kitschelt's *Logics of Party Formation* constitutes an invaluable starting point. Kitschelt examines the internal politics of ecology parties and how they shape the parties' overall strategy.[1] He explains their choices with reference to the political opportunities the parties face, and to the effects on the balance of internal factions vying to steer the new organizations—hence the logics of the title.[2] We apply Kitschelt's framework to a new national case, that of the *Verts*. That yields many anomalies, which in turn raises a number of theoretical issues.

As is the case with standard party systems theory, Kitschelt's conception of ideology and its bearing on strategy is unidimensional. Parties shift their strategies by moving along a single scale, toward either radicalism on one hand, or adaptation to and accommodation to the system on the other. In an implicit nod to Michels, Kitschelt holds that ecology parties were generally more successful and stable when they chose cooperation and alliance favored by pragmatists over the autonomy and radicalism of ideologues.[3] Choosing a unilinear ideological scale, he ignores the considerable ideological variation between otherwise similiar ecology parties. Arguing that only a cooperative strategy is rational, Kitschelt overlooks the possibility that negotiation and compromise on matters of principle can blur the party's political identity (and thus the seriousness of those who fight it within ecology parties). Positing, in effect, a single rational strategy, Kitschelt forecloses discussion of the dynamics of competition between parties, and the varying types of strategies that may be appropriate in different situations.

The Logics of Party Formation does deal with ideology, insofar as it examines a type of party with a characteristic ideological profile. Kitschelt calls these "left/libertarian parties," since they value socially progressive goals and decentralized political forms.[4] The main axis of conflict within them, however, appears to be the means the party uses to advance whatever ends it happens to seek, not the ends themselves. Factions within left-libertarian parties are either ideological or they are not; they reject compromise or do not. It is as though there is no conflict within as to what these ideologies are really about. Yet the conflict over the relative importance of "red" and "green" demands is just as essential to ecological politics as the conflict over whether or not to compromise and adapt to established political institutions and parties.

Since Kitschelt's analysis does not take into account such variation in goals, it follows that there are no terms for explaining the
variation. Kitschelt does examine the left/libertarian parties' alliance strategies from election to election, and, interestingly, the
prospective ally always seems to be a mainstream socialist party.
But this fact is never raised to the level of a theme for comparative investigation. We shall argue that the success of earlier tries
at alliance and convergence with socialists, and the reserve of
trust or suspicion that result, affects the prevailing attitude
within the greens toward socialist principles themselves—that is,
the choice of "red" versus "green." In fact, the imperatives of *inter*-
party competition, rather than *intra*-party competition, may have
more power to explain the long-range patterns of variance in the
Grüne and *Vert* strategies.[5] The French ecologists thus built their
identity, after years of mutual antagonism, upon the failures of
French Socialism. The German Greens assumed, fatefully, that
their alliance partner, the SPD was too thoroughly embroiled in
the management of capitalism to ever surpass them as the champions of environmental and social reform.

We therefore propose to incorporate the iterated games of so-
cialist/green competition as an alternative to Kitschelt's more diachronic framework, which focuses on the greens alone in single
elections. We also observe, in light of the French case, that there
are situations where radical strategies, stressing ideological and
political autonomy—strategies of identity—are rational in some
situations. We discuss first Kitschelt's classification (the descrip-
tive features that identify different tendencies within ecology parties), and then his typology (the framework for explaining the
relative strength of each tendency), with reference to the views
and historical experience of the *Grünen* and *Verts*.

I
The Logics of Party Formation:
Classifying Ecology Party Factions

Grüne Factions

Kitschelt identifies three characteristic political tendencies in
green parties, each with a distinct view of the strategic course
the party ought to take.[6] "Ideologues" want comprehensive social

change ("collective goods"), and believe that incremental gains only diminish the parties' drive to effect this type of change. They are strongly committed to working alongside autonomous citizens' movements, emphasize public consciousness-raising, and regard routine parliamentary and electoral competition as inimical to those values and aims. "Pragmatists" want collective goods as well. But pragmatists, by definition, want results, and they are far more willing to use incremental means to achieve them. Thus they accept practices of normal political competition—coalitions, bargaining, and expedient compromises—because they believe that these are the best means to achieve the ends the party seeks. Unlike either ideologues or pragmatists, a third category, "lobbyists," do not seek comprehensive reform at all. Instead, these favor very particular causes. Lobbyists seek specific rewards for particular constituencies.[7]

It is interesting that Kitschelt introduces some other patterns of internal divisions within the *Grünen* that do not correspond to his scheme comprising pragmatists, ideologues, and lobbyists.[8] In addition to pragmatists and ideologues, we learn that there are also "ecosocialists" and "ecolibertarians." These are identified, furthermore, by the content of their demands rather than their means of realizing them. Characterizing these additional currents will be invaluable when we compare *Grüne* and *Verts* factions below.[10] Ecosocialists placed primacy on the socioeconomic sphere in explaining environmental degradation. Echoing Marxist theory, they tended to interpret the ecological crisis as one manifestation of a deeper crisis of capitalism.[11] Accordingly, ecosocialists wished to fuse socialized ownership with more ecologically sound forms of material production. In addition, they were more likely than some of their counterparts to advocate internal party hierarchy, and, in the same vein, features of a planned economy.[11] Ecolibertarians stood at the opposite end of the ideological spectrum from ecosocialists. In their view, social issues were of secondary importance to the detrimental effects of industrial production itself. They rejected the egalitarian outlook and statist instruments of socialism, either Eastern or Western, calling for "reduced production, less state involvement, fewer promises, fewer applications of technical know-how, etc."[12] They argued instead that Western forms of parliamentary democracy are the most effective means of guaranteeing the safety of the environment. Ecolibertarians' choice of political partners reflected this outlook: they rejected alliances with the SPD, and viewed the Christian Democratic parties more favorably.[13] The third group, the radical ecologists, saw environmentalism as a wholly new and distinct ideology, and valued movement-centered symbolic action more than realpolitik and tactical maneuvering.[14] The fourth are the "realos," or realists, who closely resemble a pure type in Kitschelt's framework, the pragmatists.

Kitschelt winds up collapsing these four categories into his two ideal factional types. He holds that ecosocialists tended to side with radical ecologists to compose the fundi wing, comprising what Kitschelt would classify as the party ideologues. Radicals tended to side with ecosocialists because both want comprehensive systemic change. Conversely, ecolibertarians are closer to the more pragmatic realos, because both accept existing social and institutional arrangements. Yet one of these new subtypes, the ecosocialists, looms larger within the constellation of tendencies in the *Grünen* than Kitschelt lets on. Allied with radical ecologists in the *Grüne* Federal Executive, ecosocialists prepared the party's programmatic platforms—and thus had a central role in defining its political identity.[15] The ecolibertarians, in contrast, represented a small minority at national party congresses during the 1980s and were influential only in the state of Baden-Wurttemburg.[16]

Further, the ecosocialist sensibility or ideological framework cut across divisions over instrumental strategy. There were ecosocialist realos as well as fundis, including academics such as Claus Offe and Helmut Wiesenthal, and parliamentarian Otto Schily. There were close ties in culture, political background, and policies between these activists and the Left wing of the SPD. If these activists advocated coalition with the Social Democrats, it was not necessarily out of a cynical incrementalism. Rather, they believed that, as the main party of the working class, the SPD was the only political force sufficient to move West German society toward a green, yet socialized, political economy.[17] Furthermore, ecosocialism appears still more important by virtue of its relative absence from the views of any *Vert* factions. If we try to pair up *Verts* and *Grüne* factions, we find many parallels. Yet the differences among the very same groups on other criteria are quite as striking. The more the dissonance grates, the more critical for Kitschelt's framework.

Verts vs. *Grünen*: "Ideologues"

Within the *Verts*, one group clearly merited the label ideologues. They were called *"integristes"* (fundamentalists),[18] "khmers verts"[19] "ninistes" (based on their slogan that ecology should remain "ni droite/ ni gauche"—neither Right nor Left). To distinguish them from analogous *Grüne* factions, we refer to them as Waechterians, after Antoine Waechter, their intellectual father, reigning party spokesperson, and the party's most visible media figure between 1986 until December 1993. There are striking similarities between this group and the radical ecologist "fundis"— the ideologues of the *Grünen*. Both adopted many elements of the identity strategy.

Both *Vert* and *Grüne* ideologues placed priority on their parties' ties to independent social movements and denigrated institutionalized politics. The late Petra Kelly, spokesperson from 1980 to 1983, *Bundestag* member from 1983 to 1990, and a member of the radical ecologist wing, coined the term *antiparty party* for the *Grünen*, arguing that it was a movement and not a party.[20] Radical ecologists advocated a "two-legged strategy," with which the parliamentary party would, in a metaphor with soccer, serve as a "spielbein" [kicking leg] or propaganda arm of the wider grassroots movement [the "standbein" or standing leg].[21] Anything that signalled the transformation of the *Grünen* into what was called a "stinknormal" (i.e, "stinkingly mundane") party was feared and stoutly resisted. Radical ecologists called for an abrupt social transformation. Former East German dissident Rudolph Bahro, a member of the Federal Executive from 1982 to 1984, spoke for this current of thought within the *Grünen* when he demanded a "radical U-turn away from industrial society."[22] Jutta Ditfurth proposed the alternative: an "easily surveyable, communicative, convivial community amenable to self-management."[23]

The Waechterians had close personal ties to the grassroots environmental movement.[24] Like the *Grüne* radical ecologists, the pure ecologists held closely to the aims and values associated with that movement and believed that it represented their party's most viable base of political support.[25] Like *Grüne* radical ecologists, they looked at all social and political affairs through the lens of the environmental crisis. In a speech at a *Vert* party assembly in 1986, Antoine Waechter noted gravely that "[the] environmental crisis is unfortunately before us," which carried the more positive corollary that the environmental movement had a dynamic future in store for it.[26] Like their counterparts in the *Grünen*, Waechterians were inclined to view industrial society and the powers that guide it as uniformly depraved, allowing scarcely a shaft of daylight. To Waechter, opposing the municipal council in his native town of Mulhouse was equally as dehumanizing as battling the French Nuclear Authority: "the feeling of dashing myself against a wall, of having no power over events, the impression of being subject to the totalitarian effects of a closed system revolted me."[27]

Green ideologues saw the political Left and Right as morally equivalent and rejected any form of compromise with either one. *Grüne* fundamentalists attacked efforts to participate in governments with the SPD, notably in Hesse in 1985, since they felt that the more established party had betrayed the youth movement and the nuclear cause. They wanted to resist assumptions that the SPD was their natural partner, since they feared being manipulated or absorbed. Where they "tolerated" SPD governments as *Landtag* deputies (that is, voted for legislation on a case-by-case basis) fundamentalists tended to issue "non-negotiable demands" to be granted in exchange. The Waechterians also sought to steer the *Verts* away from electoral and governing alliances. Waechter coined the slogan, repeated constantly, that "ecology does not have to marry." Having voted for François Mitterrand in the presidential elections of 1981, Waechter had never forgotten the turnarounds that came soon after. Hence, *Vert* pure ecologists continually denounced the pragmatists for even proposing electoral alliances and roundly refused offers from other parties (the PS made such offers in 1989, 1992, and 1993). Regarding participation in governments, the Waechterians demanded nonnegotiable contracts, as *Grüne* radical ecologists did.

Ideologues favored a radical communicative strategy: they emphasized changing ideas as much as changing government and policy. Bahro advanced the idea of forming a "radical majority" committed to green principles through action entirely outside the parliamentary and electoral arena. The Greens, Bahro argued, needed to sway public opinion before they could ever govern successfully; barring that, compromises would be self-defeating. Many fundamentalists like Bahro, Kelly, and Ditfurth hoped that a solution to current problems lay in experiments in communal living and green lifestyles. That in turn would depend on individuals' willingness to transform their own lives in this direction. Waechter, too, called for a "revolution in mentalities," which he thought could secure popular participation in environmental action. The pure ecologists justified their strict nonaligned position by arguing that their party was working to form a "cultural majority," which might eventually allow it to govern independently. Finally, while Waechter did not explicitly advocate utopian experiments, he made many references to the attachment to one's native culture as an innate human drive, and pointed to the need for a more decentralized structure of society.

Despite these parallels, the differences between *Grüne* and *Vert* ideologues were just as striking. The two diverged in their views of the ideals and existing models of socialism. If *Grüne* radicals did not go so far as to advocate a transition to a Soviet-style socialist state, they were tepid in their opposition to it up until the time of German unification (with the exception of Bahro, a political refugee from the East).[28] Further, the fundis' model for an antiparty party was actually a West European-style Communist Party (an entity conspicuously absent from the Federal Republic's party system, as opposed to that of France). The decentralized society that fundamentalist greens such as Difurth advocated resembled an ecological, self-managed form of socialism.[29] Ditfurth had been active in the Communist splinter groups (K-Gruppen) that emerged in the Federal Republic in the 1970s, and was known for her explicit opposition to capitalism. Markovits and Gorski note that even when some of the more radical Greens shed their overt Marxist principles, their apocalyptic vision still echoed Marxist eschatology: the ecological crisis was a clear sign of an inevitable and final collapse of capitalism.[30]

In contrast, the Waechterian ideologues in the *Verts* labored to suppress any socialist-inspired content—whether utopian socialism, Soviet-style socialism, or even that of the French Socialist Party. If Waechter and his circle sought purity, leftist doctrine equalled contamination. Waechter, for example, charged that the *Grünen*'s losses in the first all-German elections of 1990 stemmed from the fact that their leftist ideology was by then outdated.[31] While the Waechterians predominated, the only overtures the *Verts* made to other parties or political groups were to groups seeking regional or cultural autonomy. All this stands in sharp contrast with radical ecologists within the *Grünen*, who had, after all, formed an alliance with dogmatic ecosocialists, and who hailed from the far Left.[32] In many respects, Waechterians resembled *Grüne* ecolibertarians more than *Grüne* radical ecologists. Both rejected Marxism, stressed popular participation and administrative decentralization, and tacitly accepted a market format in political economy.

Vert vs. *Grüne*: "Pragmatists"

Unlike ideologues in either party, *Vert* and *Grüne* pragmatists favored any action that could bring immediate results for the environment. It was assumed that ecology's aims were well understood by the public, and that there was broadly based support for environmental policy. Pragmatists saw no moral conflict in the power that comes with that political mandate: that is precisely what would bring the results they sought. Realo leader Joschka Fischer is one of the *Grünen*'s most widely recognized figures next to Petra Kelly and now the de facto leader of the party. Fischer argued that taking a single step in ameliorating the ecological crisis justified the party's existence, and that adherence to principles for their own sake was self-defeating.[33] Similarly, Yves Cochet, a *Vert* spokesperson from 1984 to 1986, and now a deputy in the French Parliament, argued that, though ecology was on the ascendant, they had to maintain their voters' sympathy by showing "maturity" and the willingness to govern.[34]

Vert and *Grüne* pragmatists leaned toward efficacy: they saw a clear connection between viable electoral scores and their ability to deliver the political goods in negotiations. Fischer, remarking on the *Grünen*'s disastrous experience in the 1990 all-German election debacle, observed that the regional Green parties in the Land parliaments that had made the most extensive compromises fared well even when the national party suffered such a major setback.[35] Cochet saw electoral payoffs in cooperating with the Left, since most of the greens' supporters would tend to vote for the Left in the second turn of elections in a case where no ecologist remains.[36]

Pragmatists in both parties have backed up this rhetoric of cooperation and responsibility by negotiating and accepting alliances. Fischer was Environment Minister in the SPD government in Hesse until 1987, and again after 1991. Taking stock of the major recent success of the Greens and the failure for the SPD in the October 1994 *Bundestag* elections, Fischer and other realists expressed interest in a CDU/Green alliance. Pragmatists in the *Verts* have also favored alliances with other parties, though mainly leftist ones. While he headed the party majority before 1986, Cochet and the left-ecologists proposed a "symbolic" alliance with Trotskyists, Maoists, and remnants of the PSU in 1984. They helped to arrange a conference of New Left parties and groups in 1985. They participated in a forum for the New Left, the ecologists, and identity-based movements known as the *Appel pour une Arc-en-Ciel* (Rainbow Alliance) in 1987. Cochet sponsored a motion titled "Let Us Enter Politics," which called for an electoral contract with the Socialists, in that same year. The left-ecological majority led by Dominique Voynet after November 1993 advocated a dialogue on a programmatic accord with what they saw as the most progressive forces of the Left, such as PCF reformers and members of the left wing of the PS.

Despite the parallels, there are as many irregularities in the comparison between *Vert* and *Grüne* pragmatists as there are between *Vert* and *Grüne* ideologues. The contrast becomes clear when we focus on programs and ideologies rather than on instrumental strategy. *Verts* pragmatists were usually referred to as the left wing of the *Verts* because they favored accord with the Socialist Party and those to its Left. In addition, pragmatists like Cochet steered the *Verts* in a left-ecological direction when they held the majority in the party before 1986, emphasizing socioeconomic themes such as unemployment and *autogestion* (worker self-management).

Yet *Vert* left-ecologists did not stand as far to the Left as most *Grünen*, even pragmatic ones. They were less inclined to favor items from the socialist agenda or its themes—for example, nationalizations, planning, partisanship of the industrial working class, discourse about class conflict, and opposition to capitalism—than *Grüne* ecosocialists. Unlike *Grüne* pragmatists, proposals for alliances with, or contacts between, ecology and the trade unions have never been a priority for *Vert* pragmatists. The latter have been unwilling to propose an alternative utopia on the communal socialist model, as *Grüne* radical ecologists have done.[37] *Vert* pragmatists like Cochet tacitly accept the operations of the free market.[38] If the Cochet/Voynet faction is in some way leftist, it is more "rose" (the color symbol of the French Socialist Party) than "red." Their position represents an ecological-minded version of a tradition of French Republican Socialism that addresses socioeconomic justice but not specifically working-class/management conflicts.

Beneath the chaos of factional nuances we have deliberately stirred up there is an underlying pattern. There are not one, but two dimensions of ecological factional cleavage. One concerns the attitude of a party or portion thereof toward the industrial workers' movement, or socialist programmatic material such as shifts in ownership or a socially active state. The other turns on whether a given faction supported or opposed political or electoral alliances with other parties (Kitschelt's main criterion). The factions in the two parties are arranged in these two dimensions in table 4.1. The factions appear in descending order according to their support for political alliances of any kind (the left-hand column), and for socialist themes (the right-hand column). Clearly, the overlapping cleavages crystallized in unique ways in each distinct faction. Pairs that placed close together on the first dimension are opposed on the second (e.g., Waechterians and radical ecologists, in the *Verts* and *Grünen*, respectively) or vice versa (e.g., *Vert* pragmatists and Waechterians). In addition, Waechterians and *Grüne* ecolibertarians are close in both dimensions. Finally, with respect to the ideological dimension, there is a significant variation *across* national cases, more than within them.

Table 4.1

FAVOR ALLIANCES	SUPPORT SOCIALIST THEMES
Grüne realos	Dogmatic *Grüne* socialists
Vert pragmatists	*Grüne* radical ecologists
Moderate *Grüne* ecosocialists	Moderate *Grüne* ecosocialists
Grüne ecolibertarians	*Grüne* realos
Dogmatic *Grüne* ecosocialists	*Vert* pragmatists
Vert Waectherians	*Vert* Waechterians
Grüne radical ecologists	*Grüne* ecolibertarians

All of the factions in the *Grünen* (minus ecolibertarians) may be more "red" than any in the *Verts*. The evidence suggests that Kitschelt collapses distinctive dimensions of instrumental strategy and ideology into a simple opposition between ideologues and pragmatists. The fact that so many salient cleavages cut through Kitschelt's classification scheme emerge should alert us to problems in his typology. If factional divisions do turn on "red" vs. "green," what features of the strategic situation bring them out? Why do they seem to vary together within one national case and separately across cases? Even if we accept that the basic classification ought to rest on a distinction between ideologues and pragmatists, do Kitschelt's expectations as to which will prevail hold for the case of the *Verts*?

II
Applying Kitschelt's Explanatory Framework: *Grüne* and *Vert* in Party Competition

The Logics of Party Formation argues that changes in the political system in which the ecology parties compete shapes the balance of power inside them. The "strategic situation" which parties encounter affects the relative strength of different factional groups, and that decides the party's position overall. Features of the strategic situation are the "mobilization of the cleavage on which the party is based" (i.e., the level of popular opinion supporting or opposed to the party's demands); the openness or closure of the political opportunity structure (i.e., whether formal institutions or the leading parties favor the party's participation in alliances or governments); and the ecology party's electoral competitiveness (i.e., its levels of votes relative to other parties).[39] This complex array of independent factors yields many partial combinations and particular outcomes. Nevertheless, some of them may vary together. For example, when the ecologists become more competitive, the political opportunity structure becomes more open, since elites will try to recapture their lost votes by addressing the greens' themes or making alliance offers. On the other hand, where elites reject the greens' demands, disaffected supporters may become highly mobilized in opposition. The main variable in Kitschelt's framework, then, seems to be the openness of the polity or system to the green's participation and demands, or alternately, its closure to them.

The ecologists respond to these varying conditions with one of two strategic alternatives. The party may choose either a "logic of constituency representation"—that is, by opting for support from social movements and maximal change—or a "logic of party competition"—by moving toward normal parliamentary participation, construction of electoral majorities, and compromises.[40] Where the system is closed, a logic of constituency representation holds. The general public has to be made more aware of the need for change; pressure on elites must be maintained; commitment to purity within the party organization must be secured. Ideologues tend to insist on those aims, and the party will support their objectives. Where the system is more open, pragmatists prevail instead. An electoral mandate indicates substantial support for the greens' issues, elites suddenly start to appreciate the green's ideas and demands, and thus the green's own opportunities to negotiate increase. "Lobbyists," by the way, represent a swing force: they side alternately with ideologues, or pragmatists, depending on whether the political process promises to reject or to accept the discrete causes they favor. While lobbyists' choices affect the number of supporters for one strategy or another, they do not represent an independent strategic tendency. The fundamental axis of conflict is whether or not the party should adapt to the political system; lobbyists align with whatever side suits their agenda.

Kitschelt's explanatory framework clearly fits the strategic profile of the German ecology party. The *Grünen* were highly competitive between the 1983 and 1987 *Bundestag* elections, winning first 5.6 percent, then 8.7 percent of the national vote. Political elites became somewhat more responsive, the SPD made several offers of alliances in the *Länder*, and the Greens accepted some of them.[41] After about 1987, the realos assumed a de facto position of leadership within the parliamentary party and in many *Länder*. Kitschelt's argument also holds for the *Verts* during the years immediately following the founding of the party. The French political system was closed after 1981 when the Socialists came to power. The PS governments abandoned many earlier promises regarding environmental policy. Yet the party's electoral power crowded out openings for a postindustrial challenger. In this hostile environment, therefore, it is not surprising that ideologues eventually took over the *Verts'* leadership in November 1986. By stressing its purity and distance from the corrupt status quo, the Waechterians elevated their party's very isolation to the status of a cardinal virtue.

After that point, however, events do not correspond to Kitschelt's expectations. The French political system became more open to ecology after 1988 as the *Verts* began to make inroads into the leading parties' scores. That made political elites more responsive to their demands: Lalonde entered the cabinet of the Rocard government as Secretary of State for the Environment, and the PS made repeated offers of electoral alliance contracts to the *Verts* between 1989 and 1993. Yet even in this situation, the ideologues maintained their predominance in the ecology party. The Waechterians consistently rejected the alliance offers. In addition, electoral support stabilized and even expanded through the succeeding period, between 1988 and 1992, all while the ideologues maintained their hold on the party. The next year, the two competing ecological organizations, the *Verts* and GE, adopted an allied but politically independent position, forming the *Entente Écologiste* in late 1992 to contest the parliamentary elections in March of the next year.

Why should "ideologues" and their typical strategy prevail when, according to Kitschelt, they should not have? Why did they consistently reject the temptation to cooperate with the mainstream Left? A closer examination of the history of the *Verts'* prospective ally suggests an answer. At a point when the *Verts* first became competitive, the PS commanded a significant number of left-leaning votes, and had controlled either the government or the presidency or both for seven years (i.e., in 1988). Despite its poor record on environmental policy, the PS had been quite "open," in Kitschelt's terms, to many of the postindustrial themes the greens tend to address. In fact, the PS's capacity and inclination to co-opt some of the ecologists' key themes was what had pushed the latter to the political fringes for many years. Furthermore, in the seven years the PS had held power, it had first tried, then retreated from an extraordinarily left-wing program of demand stimulation and nationalization. After that point, no small party could easily incorporate typical socialist proposals without addressing what they would do differently. More than the German Greens, therefore, the *Verts* had reasons to fear that their identity would be blurred by the socialist party in their country.

The Waechterian strategy, stressing ecology's distance from French Socialism, fit this situation. They presented a clear alternative to the ruling party when it began to suffer the contradictions of holding power. The institutions that had presented obstacles to the environmental movement or the ecology party—France's closed administrative structure, majoritarian ballot institutions, and the privileges to an entrenched political class that resulted—had clearly benefited the Socialists by that point. Therefore the *Verts* could implicate the PS, and by extension, socialism itself, in the negative aspects of these institutions. We now suggest the implications of the French case for Kitschelt's framework.

III
Toward Party Competition: The Logic of Party Formation Reexamined

Kitschelt's perspective on the ecologists and the ways they form their strategies is that of a single organization looking out at its whole environment, the constellation of political institutions and actors that tends either to facilitate or to constrain their maneuvers. Party strategies either favor cooperation and adaptation to the system or reject it, depending on the opportunities it poses for them to gain. With this approach, Kitschelt moves in the direction of generality and abstraction. This is reflected in his research design. Kitschelt's empirical study of the ecologists' strategic actions is diachronic, as we noted above.[42] Data are coded and aggregated for tests in a series of one-shot games (i.e., outcomes of single elections), multiplying the number of cases sampled. This methodological choice has important analytic consequences. One risks losing sight of the substantive issues around which competition turns, the continuous political process that shapes them, and the strategic interaction between one party and another—central concerns of classic party systems theory.

There is an admirable degree of deductive force to Kitschelt's framework. Pragmatists accept compromise, and therefore they prevail in conditions that demand compromise. Ideologues are associated with conditions that foster party integrity and purity, such as elite intransigence or political isolation. Yet the dichotomy between compromise vs. autonomy, or between conservatives and radicals, can be found in many parties, including those that have little else in common with the greens (e.g., Tory "wets" and Thatcherites). The specificity of the greens—their ideas, demands, and strategies—seems to have fallen out of focus. Of course, the conflict over alliance strategy is a particularly significant (and often debilitating) feature of the internal life of ecology parties. Even if we accept that much, we should still ask, over what is compromise to take place? and with whom?

Further, by defining factional types around the question as to whether they seek compromise or autonomy, Kitschelt forces contrasting factional types from our two cases into the same conceptual box. If ideologues seek collective goods, which collective goods are they? German fundis advocated some kind of socialization of ownership, whereas Waechterians preferred administrative decentralization and cultural autonomy. Both rejected cooperation with the mainstream Left. The former, however, did so out of disappointment with the political Left's betrayal of genuine socialist ideals. The latter opposed these ideals themselves. In other words, factions within ecology parties stake their positions around the view of the socialist party itself as much as around questions of alliance or compromise in the abstract.

Kitschelt argues that the greens fare better, in electoral terms, when they move in the direction of compromise and adaptation to the political system—that is, when they follow the logic of electoral competition.[43] In that case, the logic of constituency representation, or emphasis on the aims and values of a radical social movement, would hardly ever be logical. Yet that assertion would in turn contradict the facts of the *Verts'* case. As we shall see, the latter stumbled only when they abandoned a logic of constituency representation. The *Verts* shed their image as the representatives of the grassroots environmental movement and their emphasis on ideological fundamentals when they allied with GE and Lalonde, the consummate pragmatist—with cataclysmic results.

To address these problems, we need to look more closely at the ways that the prospective ally—inevitably the leading socialist party—shapes the greens' strategic choices. Further, we need to take a broader time frame, examining the record of previous tries at alliance or compromise and its impact on the greens' identity as they begin to establish themselves fully in the party system. The outcome of previous games can diminish uncertainty, leading to trust or, in the case of the *Verts*, to mistrust. Certain features of the socialist party in question may or may not foster trust over time: for example, its electoral strength, its party system position, the particular policies it advocates, and its record of policy achievements. Thus, in our literature review, we advanced a more dynamic alternative to Kitschelt's diachronic model. Whereas Kitschelt focuses on one-shot games, we proposed to examine iterated competitive games to explain the varying patterns in coalition strategy and ideological discourse on the part of the greens.

As the case of the *Verts* will show, attention to the history of earlier alliances would tell us why a fundamentalist, noncooperative strategy in new parties might actually be rational in some situations. Given that earlier relations with the prospective socialist ally led to mistrust, a fundamentalist line could keep its hold on the ecology party, as it and its leaders bid higher and higher for the sake of delivering real concessions. Given that this ally might be judged untrustworthy by a portion of the electorate receptive to progressive themes, a fundamentalist strategy could win sizable support by providing an authentic and clear electoral choice. Voters cannot judge new parties solely on the basis of whether or not they promise to cooperate with established parties alone. We need to pay more attention, then, to what draws voters toward the new parties, as much as what pushes them away from the established ones. We should ask what ends they propose to achieve, not just what means they propose to realize them.

The strength and ideological position of the socialist party are the main factors determining the ways that ecologists frame those ideological ends. Since it has superior electoral strength, greater penetration of political institutions, and is committed to explicit programs of government, the leading socialist party's position will be fairly constant over time. Thus we should expect to see definite strategic patterns that are common to the whole ecological organization during the same time. We would accordingly not expect to see factional balances oscillate rapidly between extremes of ideological or pragmatic strategies, as Kitschelt's diachronic approach might suggest. The ecological faction that can prove, through a series of elections, that it has the most viable competitive strategy may ultimately shape the identity of the party. This is why *Vert* and *Grüne* factions, whatever their tactical differences, seem to vary together within the parties and apart across the two national cases: the pure ecologists and ecosocialists, respectively, put their stamp on the ideological profile of their party. Interparty competition may thus be more decisive than intraparty competition in understanding this ideological and strategic formation over time, and factional accord more pronounced than factional conflict. In the next chapter, we examine the red/green and pure green identities around which factional competition turned, and which defined the ecologists' position within their political systems.

Chapter *Five*

Contrasting Images of Ecological Politics: The Programs of the *Verts* and *Grünen* in Comparative Perspective

Introduction: Framing Environmental Demands

Like all ideologies of progressive reform, the political programs of the *Grünen* and *Vert* ideologies hold up a mirror to some central problem in contemporary society to project an image of a more just alternative. Both depart from a critique of productivism: that is, the unquestioned value placed on material growth without regard to its consequences, and without democratic means for deciding who shall be affected. In the productivist model, politics does not address the consequences or value of production. Neither the representatives of organized labor and management, nor the parties of the Left and Right, question the productivist system itself. They simply struggle over its fruits. As a solution, both parties aimed to politicize the process of production by opening it up to popular deliberation and choice. With more control over the affairs that impacted on their lives, individuals would take more care to safeguard the environment, and see the personal benefits in greater involvement in the life of their communities.[1]

If we look further, however, the *Grünen* focus on the material side of this formula. They propose to democratize the sphere of work and industrial production itself. The *Verts'* version places emphasis on the procedural side. It identifies the types of institutions that can submit questions about growth and the environment to greater public debate and allow individuals more self-management. This chapter will show how these contrasting emphases inform comprehensive yet distinct models of environmental, social, and political reform. We draw the evidence from campaign platforms and statements, programmatic motions from internal party congresses or meetings, as well as published writings that party leaders or activists have used to clarify their positions.[2] The materials were produced as the *Grünen* and *Verts* first began to define themselves and compete successfully with the socialist parties by advancing red/green and pure ecological identities, respectively (i.e., from 1980 to 1987, in the case of the *Grünen*; and 1988 to 1993, for the *Verts*). We shall deal with the subtle shifts that have recently taken place in the ecologists' agendas later on, after we have fully examined this formative period in their programmatic development.

In "Critical Perspectives on Contemporary Society," we ask how the parties view deficiencies in the market economy or the nation/state. The *Grüne* version interprets power as economic power, and sees the potential for domination resting in control over production processes. It follows that the route toward a greener society would be to shift control over production processes to those most directly affected by it. The state, we should note, is tacitly considered to be a positive force for such change. In the *Grüne* agenda, the existing state apparatus is suspect only insofar as it upholds the capitalist order. Because of the influence of Marxism, and of elements of Keynes's thought adopted by European social democrats, the *Grüne* program resembled that of the Left of the SPD at around the same time.

The *Verts'* program, more anarchist than Marxist, opposes not only economic hierarchy but hierarchy-as-such, whether it be geopolitical, bureaucratic, sexual, or cultural. The fundamental problem in current forms of social organization is that those in superior positions grow remote from information about environmental problems and detached from the interests of the majority immediately affected. The solution is decentralized politics, not decentralized production. Decisions about environmental issues should be made at a political or administrative level that is as close to the issues and actors involved as possible.[3] Viewed in this light, the highly centralized contemporary nation/state, built on conquest and exploitation of natural resources, is unambiguously negative. The *Verts'* program is far more likely to implicate the socialist Left, both Eastern and Western, in this centralizing project.

In "Emancipatory Projects," we examine the particular areas each program targets for reform, and the social benefits they believe will result from it. The *Grüne* program ties individual improvement and self-realization to more meaningful and healthy work, and proposes the decentralization of the workplace to achieve it. The *Vert* program focuses more on participation in politics than in the workplace, and on the formal institutions or territorial units that can promote it. In the *Vert* version, the devolution of power to smaller, more autonomous units is part of an explicitly global or international project for environmental change. The *Grüne* version is more centered on the domestic (i.e., German) arena, particularly the economy. We close this chapter by foreshadowing the strategic implications of each programmatic alternative.

I
Critical Perspectives on Contemporary Society: the Economy

Die Grünen: The Ecological Critique of Capitalism

In Marx's account of the political and social relations of capitalism, the aim of industrial production is profit and not socially useful value. Work is organized according to narrow criteria of efficiency, and that diminishes the subjective powers or basic needs of the immediate producers themselves. Capital's control over the organization of work accords it a preponderant share of power in the social sphere. Owners of capital represent a center of social power that must be vigorously opposed, generally through the agency of a strong state apparatus. Social relations cannot be fundamentally transformed by action in the representative political sphere, which allows only incremental change at best, and at worst defeats truly emancipatory reforms.[4]

The *Grünen's* 1980 Federal Program echoes each one of these strands in classic Marxist thought. Section II, titled "Economy and Work," is accorded the honor of first place after the Preamble. Power is concentrated in the hands of capital: "the ecological balance is sacrificed to the aspiration for economic growth and improved prospects for competitiveness and profit."[5] Workplace conditions under this system are alienating and dehumanizing. In addition to the spoilage of the physical environment, workers suffer ever increasing mental and physical demands, and technological change proceeds without attention to their needs or well-being. The established parties reinforce or perpetuate the social asymmetries which the profit motive generates, and their chief aim is to reinforce ecologically destructive economic growth. This fundamental critique of capitalism is joined with radical proposals to transform it, such as calls for a total ban on ecologically harmful industries.[6]

The *Grüne* critique of contemporary industrial society addresses many areas of economic life and social relations outside the workplace or industrial relations. In these matters as well, there are parallels with Marx. Areas of consumption or work outside the factory are still understood as secondary spheres of social relations that function to reproduce the primary sphere of industrial production. The advertising industry, for example, is a key mediator between the spheres of factory production on one hand, and the culture of consumption on the other.[7] Appealing to the most hedonistic impulses of consumers, advertising instills an illusory sense of satisfaction and feeds the demand for industrial products.[8] Therefore advertising feeds the quantitative growth of the consumer economy and perpetuates the huge volume of waste that it entails. In another instance of their characteristically maximalist position with respect to the pace of reform, the *Grünen* demand a ban on ecologically harmful advertising, and its outright exclusion from publicly owned media.[9]

In the *Grüne* program, oppressed groups are defined by their position in the workforce and their level of disposition over economic resources. There is a substantial list of feminist demands. But the oppression of women is viewed as economic oppression.

The traditional conception of the female role of housewife and mother is couched in ironic terms, implying that it is a social construction that legitimates a form of labor necessary to capitalism.[10] There are no claims that women have some privileged or essential relationship with "life" or nature (e.g., because of their closeness to reproduction or nurturing).[11] The *Grünen* simply demand that women receive better opportunities to participate in the economy and in political decisions.[12] Women's work thus secures the minimal conditions of survival for the male industrial worker to earn household wages. The lack of economic alternatives available to them allows women no latitude to pursue the alternate avenues for self-development open to men. As one solution, the *Grünen* propose to reduce the length of the work week in order to allow men to share in family chores.[13]

The *Grüne* program views the situation of the unemployed or underclass as a consequence of capital's quest for profit, and proposes vigorous measures to counter it. To offset the effects of unemployment or underemployment, the *1980 Federal Program* calls for a guaranteed subsistence income.[14] The Sindelfingen Conference Program of 1983 calls for additional state activity to reduce unemployment, and criticizes the trend of diminishing social expenditures.[15] The Reconstruction Program of 1986 upholds the right to a basic subsistence income, asserting that nothing less than "the abolition of social classes" was the aim. To reverse unemployment, the *Grüne* do not adopt the standard social democratic goal of full employment, however, since that would justify excessive growth (i.e., growth in the absolute number of work hours, which they opposed for its environmentally harmful side effects). Instead they propose to reduce the number of hours in the work week. That would distribute the absolute level of work hours more equitably, rather than generate more of them (the *Verts* also supported this idea, though with a very different political emphasis).

Les Verts: The Critique of Liberal Economics on Its Own Terms

To the *Verts*, work and the economy are not a privileged site for social contestation or environmental reform. The *Verts* tend to interpret socioeconomic inequality in terms of a general tendency of societies towards hierarchization. The *Vert* pamphlet on economic policy characterizes industrial hierarchy as the domination of managers over executors, not owners over proletarians. The same passage subsumes industrial hierarchy into another category, that of one gender over another. The division between worker and manager "is governed by a ruthlessly masculine vision of human action: to construct plans for a limited end, while forgetting the complexity of needs, desires, the importance of cycles of growth and maturity, and the need for care and prudence."[16]

In the area of socioeconomic change, the *Vert* program is less radical than that of the *Grünen*. When they criticize current economic practices, they tend to do so within the terms of classical economic rationality themselves. One document explicitly states that the ecologists cannot oppose economic growth in principle, since they see no other means to finance environmental protection or social programs.[17] Where the operation of the market is unjust, the corrections the *Verts* propose are meant to restore competitiveness itself, whether that of labor or business.[18] Choices as to what gets produced should be made by a consensus among interested parties: by producers as much as consumers, and by management in cooperation with labor. In the *Vert* program, the decentralization of decionmaking, not a change in control of production, would facilitate this process of consensus formation.[19]

Like the *Grünen*, the *Verts* support a program of work sharing through a reduction in the working week. Yet the latter hold that this will benefit not just the unemployed or the underemployed, but also salaried professionals as well. Each group would benefit from the increase in free time and improved productivity. The *Vert* pamphlet on the economy makes other implicitly cross-class appeals. For example, it alludes to the interests of entrepreneurs as well as consumers. Industry has an interest in securing the safety of their investment; environmentally sound products are more generally valued and lasting ones.[20] Rather than abolish the market to save the environment, the *Verts*' programs simply try to identify the most impractical allocations of existing resources, as well as depletion of finite natural resources. For example, they criticize the French Nuclear Authority, *Électricité de France* (EDF) for diseconomies of scale, and the Common Agricultural Policy of the European Community [now the European Union] for its market-distorting subsidies.[21]

II
Critical Perspectives on Contemporary
Society: The State

Die Grünen: The State and Economic Power

At times, the *1980 Federal Program* echoes Marx's tendency to view the power of the state—the government's administrative apparatus or the executive that controls it—as derived from economic power. State policy perpetuates social cleavages, in this perspective. Its policies of pricing, taxation, and subsidies actually increase income disparities.[22] The legal system is biased in favor of existing economic arrangements.[23] The German party-state, in which political parties control administrative appointments, promotes consensus only among the most economically powerful and excludes more radical voices.[24] Redistributive and welfare provisions of the German social market economy merely secure consent to the prevailing socioeconomic order and give rise to a paternalistic welfare bureaucracy. Negative effects of the welfare apparatus include unemployment, poor health care, and discrimination against women.[25]

In these passages, the state and its various branches would seem to be an alien force, inherently opposed to the public's true interests, either environmental or social.[26] It would thus follow that the German state's institutional form has to be transcended along with its capital-derived content. Certain passages draw these anarchist conclusions. The *1980 Federal Program* calls for the institution of direct democracy in the Federal Republic, and promises to maintain close contact with the grassroots movements whom they believe share this goal, including the citizens', environmental, and labor movements.[27]

Yet alongside this anarchist view of the state there runs a republican strain in *Grüne* programs. Economic power has to be restrained, and the state is the only entity with sufficient power to meet that goal. The Marxist view of the class-based nature of the state is thus tempered by the more Keynesian principle of employing state action as a corrective to capitalism's most debilitating excesses.[28] Certain passages suggest that state institutions, imbued with the authority of a popular mandate, could check whatever domestic interests or foreign powers might oppose change toward a more peaceful or environmental society. State intervention is a necessary counterweight to the interests of capital, since it may act on behalf of disadvantaged regions or portions of the population. Frankland and Schoonmaker point out that the *1980 Federal Program* implies the existence of an active state, since it proposes national agencies to enforce environmental or sexual discrimination policy, or to plan environmental land use.[29] The *Grünen*'s Reconstruction Program of 1986 proposes to restructure private industry through a combination of taxes, legal instruments, and subsidies, to provide a guaranteed wage for workers affected by these measures, and to extend public transportation and health programs—all of which imply the existence of some central entity with power and scope sufficient to realize these reforms.[30]

The *Grünen*'s opposition to capitalism leads them to imply a positive role for the state in foreign policy as much as in the domestic sphere. To the *Grünen*, capitalism—incarnated as foreign capital—is behind the militarism and geopolitical expansion all ecologists tend to deplore. American economic power, for example, inherently requires military and economic expansion.[31] The *Grünen*'s *1987 Federal Election Program* identified the United States rather than the Soviet Union as the preeminent danger to global peace and security (and particularly for those of Germany, a potential battleground in the event of superpower hostility).[32]

The *Grünen* tacitly accepted the legitimacy of the East German state and regime, both as a guarantee of peace and to support what they saw as a viable socialist alternative to Western capitalism. The *Grünen* were not oblivious to the East German state's repression of its citizens. Their prescription, however, was not to oppose the East German regime itself, but to open closer ties with it. Hence the Greens called for a dialogue between the two states on matters of peace, disarmament, and the environment. Like much of the German Left, members of the German Green Party saw the territorial division of Germany as a morally acceptable consequence of the Nazi period. The rationale was that the existence of the socialist regime in the German Democratic Republic prevents the recrudescence of German expansionism and nationalism.[33] Their East German policy was quite similar to *Ostpolitik* (Eastern Policy), advanced by the SPD during the Brandt administrations of 1969 to 1973.[34]

Les Verts: The State Paradigm of Centralization and Conquest

In contrast to the *Grünen*, the French Greens did not, and perhaps could not, view their own country's state and administrative structure in equivocal terms. The French state has been, classically, a power unto itself; hence the state itself is the problem. In contrast to the Federal Republic, built on executive restraint and weak in geopolitical terms, the contemporary French state and foreign policy were founded on principles of executive power and national autonomy. Hence the *Verts* thought that the French state was the very incarnation of the regional and international hierarchies they wanted to correct: bureaucratic domination, the arms buildup, reliance on dangerous forms of energy, North/South inequality, and of course environmental spoilage. Their programs contain a far more explicit and radical critique of state institutions, both republican and administrative.

In the *Vert* program, the state's power is not only economic, but administrative, juridical, and coercive (i.e., related to military and police functions).[35] Heads of state seek a stable international environment in order to continue to extract the resources that sustain state power (i.e., economic, natural, and, in the form of cheap labor, human resources). The exploitation of national and international resources does not necessarily serve the profit-driven motives of an entrepreneurial class, in the *Verts*' view. Rather, it serves to perpetuate the state's advantage in the international sphere, leading to the extraction of more resources, and so forth.

From the *Verts*' perspective, the state exists not so much to serve the ends of capital, but becomes an end in itself. Insulated from public demands and accountability, elites within the state tend to identify their own political and career interests more fully with its prestige and geopolitical position rather than with those of any part of the population they are mandated to serve. Where power, furthermore, is centered in one metropolitan area, the *Verts* tend to argue that the elite minority lacks the will and even the capacity to arbitrate among the complex and overlapping lines of social cleavage in contemporary society. Elite autonomy and insulation from public accountability has resulted in massive levels of official corruption and the people's utter distrust of their representatives.[36]

To the *Verts*, the French nuclear power program is a glaring example of the divide between the ends of state and those of its citizens. The legitimacy of a centralized, comprehensive nuclear power program ostensibly rests in its ability to guarantee national security, limit France's dependence on energy exporters, and provide intrinsic savings. The *Vert* document on energy policy seeks to counter these ideas, once again alluding to economic rationality as well as to moral standards. Nuclear energy is not only fraught with hazards to the population, in the *Verts'* view. Its production is costly, and its advanced technology gives rise to a secretive and self-perpetuating bureaucracy.[37] French nuclear testing in the South Pacific contradicts its populations' right to self-determination and keeps them in a perpetual state of fear.[38] In contrast to the *Grüne* perspective, *Vert* programs hold that states in Eastern Socialist societies and in Western liberal ones are morally equivalent, in environmental and political terms. Both exhibit a rapacious—and, ultimately, irrational—drive toward resource accumulation. France's electrical and nuclear authority, the EDF, and Soviet technocrats need not fear the consequences of their actions, since they will receive state funding with few qualifications. Thus, *"they value growth as an end in itself, whether they manage a 'public utility,' or 'the people's property'* [emphasis in original]."[39]

From the perspective of international relations, *Vert* programmatic documents generally consider the state to be as irrational, unjust, and obsolete as it is in the French domestic sphere. States throughout the globe are becoming contested from below, since they are unresponsive to citizen's demands. Yet they are also subject to strains from above, since they cannot solve or check the transnational forces such as pollution, immigration, or refugees. The problems are rooted in the rigid asymmetries in the economic power of the nations of the Northern and Southern Hemispheres. Advanced Northern states began long ago to extract resources and cheap labor from the South on the basis of unfair terms of exchange. Contemporary Northern investment programs in the South are geared toward economic efficiency, not ecological or social rationality. The less developed nations are forced to rely on exported forms of energy or agricultural development that are poorly adapted to tropical climates. Hence they have little choice but to turn to practices that are harmful for the global environment, such as forest depletion and desertification. Further, since developing countries nevertheless often fail to provide either subsistence or employment for their growing populations, massive migrations toward the North occur, straining social relations and political systems in the host countries.[40]

Grüne programs also contain passages on economic exploitation in the Third World and support for liberation struggles there: for example, Section II9 of the *1980 Federal Program*, entitled "Partnership with Third World Countries." That text also notes the hazards of the Western path to industrialization for the developing world, calls for more environmentally sound apportionment of economic aid, demands an end to the exploitation of cheap third world labor, and advocates the rights of ethnic minorities to cultural expression.[41] Nevertheless, the *Grünen* do not connect these proposals to any critique of the state. As we observed, they imply that the state may be a positive counterweight to international capital, and view the latter as the fundamental cause of environmental and human degradation.

III
Emancipatory Themes in
Ecological Programs

Die Grünen: Autonomy in Industrial Production

To the *Grünen*, opportunities for individual self-development stem from material well-being, and, above all, from meaningful work. The Preamble to the *1980 Federal Program* asserts that participating in an economy driven by waste is not just irresponsible but demoralizing.[42] Without the need to pursue narrow material satisfaction, individuals might place less value on material gain and put their energy into innovation and creativity instead. Further, opportunities for meaningful, dignified work must be distributed equally throughout society.[43] Promoting more humane and fulfilling work complements the social policies the *Grünen* propose, such as a guaranteed life wage, since tedious work is of course only accepted for financial reasons.[44] The *Grünen* do call for guarantees of civil and political rights, but these demands do not have near the same priority or space as they do in the *Verts'* program.[45]

If meaningful work is the goal, change must begin in the workplace.[46] In order to reform work to suit their own interests, workers would have to have control over production processes.[47] Since the immediate producers would then be responsible for and subject to the effects of their activities, industrial output would be more socially useful and ecologically sound than under the short-run logic of profit maximization. The *Grüne* program does not explicitly call for a change in the ownership of production. Yet the shifts they demand in the control over production processes themselves would significantly alter the fundamental features of capitalism, wherein decisions are made by management on the basis of the profit motive alone.

In the *Grüne* perspective, the scope and size of industrial production, not just social relations within the factory itself, would have to change. The *Reconstruction Program* calls for the dismantling of large industries, where possible, and their reorganization into small "surveyable" production units. The type of production would also change: the most harmful branches of production would cease in favor of more social and environmentally beneficial alternatives, such as renewable energy and public transport. To coordinate the changes in production, the *Grünen* propose a more radical version of the legislation for *mitbestimmung* (worker codetermination) enacted by the SPD government in the 1970s. They demand labor parity on works councils, extension of the scope of office and factory council powers to the shopfloor, the democratization of employment policy, and workers' control over investment, including investment in new technologies. Economic and social councils would replace the party/state, planning and coordinating the whole economy. Advanced computer technology, incidentally, would make these massive reforms possible: it could stem the need to increase the division of labor; allow workers to plan and design new, environmentally sound processes; and thus it would stimulate inquiry and make work more interesting.[48]

To achieve gains for working people, the *Grünen* anticipated partnership with their representatives in the trade unions. The *1980 Federal Program* calls for a political alliance with the unions, and supports their rights. These include the right to strike and to form unions; workers' rights to political activity; union participation in hiring and and wage negotiation; and protection of trade union officials from dismissal. This same section lists one goal that is inconsistent with the last demand, though in keeping with their overall push toward decentralized production: the strengthening of grassroots democracy within the unions.[49]

Les Verts: **Toward Political Autonomy**

Whereas the *Grünen* focus on the decentralization of industry, the *Verts'* project is more global in every sense. They apply the principle of decentralization to a variety of social institutions, both in domestic and international politics, and anticipate a more diverse set of emancipatory benefits. The *Verts* see enhanced political participation as one of the greatest benefits of decentralization, since it fosters self-development. With greater access to political decisions, each individual would have more incentive to get involved, see the impact of his or her actions on the community and the environment, and become more educated about competing political perspectives. Having the economic means to master one's own fate is an element of self-development, in the *Vert* program. Yet it is only one route among a diverse set of social aspirations. In the same vein, there is no single privileged ally—such as the working class—in the push for emancipatory reform. There are no references to links with trade unions. The *Verts* cite a more heterogeneous set of potential allies: regionalists, feminists, pacifists, and advocates of identity politics.[50]

Because of the importance they place on social and political diversity, it follows that the *Verts* focus on institutions that can safeguard it. Only by devolving power to smaller geographic units, they argue, can governments handle the complexity involved in a plural society, and in environmental deliberations in particular. Those affected by the outcome of the process would take at least a minimal part in deciding them. Differences can best be articulated and resolved at a level where deliberations would not lead to overload or stagnation. It is true that allowing more interested groups to gain access to political debates might be disorganized and time consuming. To the *Verts*, the legitimacy of the final outcomes would outweigh these disadvantages.[51]

Within these decentralized units, there would have to be procedural guarantees for free and open debate and mechanisms for consensus formation. Only then could groups, communities, or nations ever manage the complicated task of balancing values of environmental soundness with social equitability.[52] The *Vert* program calls for many institutional guarantees of minority rights in domestic politics, such as proportional representation in parliaments, referenda held by popular initiative, "shifting relative majorities" in legislation (i.e., voting issue by issue rather than in preestablished alliances or simple majorities). The premium on free choice holds at the international level as well. Individual nations would never adhere to international agreements if they had not entered into them freely and after full deliberation. Therefore international institutions have to be sustained and respected.[53]

Despite their tendency to favor smaller political units, the *Vert* program does acknowledge the need for some international authority that would allow them to coexist and communicate (the *Grüne* program tends to concentrate on domestic matters and on German autonomy). This follows from their view that nation/states are inadequate to the task of managing the transnational environmental and social forces of a global economy. The *Verts* thus support European integration. Although cautious about too much concentration of power in Brussels, they support building political institutions at the federal European level to coordinate and enforce environmental policy.[54] As a counterweight to power at the federal level of the European Union, the *Verts* support the idea of a "Europe of Regions," in which regions delineated by physical and cultural boundaries, sometimes those cutting across current national boundaries, would have autonomy in matters of public policy. Regional allocation of resources would lead to more responsible use, the *Verts* believe, and transportation policy would better fit local geography and demographics. Participation within these smaller cultural units that the *Verts* envision would be grounded on a shared cultural identity.[55]

The devolution of power to autonomous cultural units should not be taken to imply insularity, or worse, xenophobia. If individual regions have a right to the expression of their own local cultures, it is assumed that these rights have universal scope. In fact, the *Vert* program foresees the need for political and cultural interchange between regions. Tolerance of alien cultures is an essential feature of the individual self-development the *Verts* seek. Contact with foreign cultural perspectives stimulates understanding and innovation as much as it fosters respect for regional differences, in their view.[56]

Ideology as Strategy: Political Implications of the *Grüne* and *Vert* Programs

The red/green and pure ecological programs may represent opposite sides of the strategic dilemma we analyzed in the literature review: the tradeoff between efficacy and identity. A materialist program like the *Grünen*'s has the value of efficacy. It targets a fairly broad spectrum of social groups who may have an intense interest in change, and who can thus be mobilized to help effect reform. Environmental interests intersect with economic grievances. Economically subordinate groups, such as workers, trade unions, the unemployed, and women, might have an interest in a coalition with service sector workers seeking to secure meaningful jobs and opposing dehumanizing or harmful forms of production. The problem with this strategy is that it sacrifices identity. Proponents of a materialist version of ecology have the burden of explaining why their ideas could not be subsumed into social democratic formulae that would be, in effect, simply updated to be more sensitive to environmental concerns.

In contrast, the *Verts'* program is patterned closely on the core themes of the environmental movement, such as decentralization and political diversity, without the incorporation of other ideas, such as those of Marxism or social democracy in the case of the *Grünen*. It emphasizes identity and purity, perhaps to the detriment of efficacy. The strategic problem for the *Verts* is that it is not clear who, outside the most active elements of the environmental movement, might be expected to identify with these themes enough to support them reliably. Building their identity around environmental issues pure and simple, the ecologists may risk being seen as a single issue movement, and may lack credibility and stature when they try to build bridges to other forces and their characteristic issues. With a grasp of the ideas behind the *Grüne* and *Vert* strategies, we can now begin to consider how they perform in practice. To understand why they chose the contrasting directions in the first place, we examine certain founding moments in the greens' development and the competitive constraints they faced.

Chapter *Six*

Entering the Political Arena:
Strategic Cues and False Starts

Emerging Forms from Primordial Chaos

The first small ecology parties to form in France and Germany had little of the ideological cement needed to form permanent parties with coherent strategies. These early ecological lists or prototype green parties not only had no unifying ideology; they lacked the resources or formal structures to disseminate it. In each case, the greens only developed a clear, coherent ideology later, once they formed permanent national organizations—the *Grünen* and *Verts*—out of this inchoate mix of prototype parties and began to compete regularly with other parties. That underscores our claim that ideology is strategic for the ecologists: choices of programmatic material are formed by their need to define their identities vis-à-vis their competitors.

We begin our empirical study of green/socialist competition, then, by noting the heterogeneous nature of the first ecological electoral lists and prototype parties that formed as offshoots of the grassroots environmental movement around 1976 in both countries. After that, we find that positive scores correlate with a strategy that successfully addresses that of the socialist party. The SPD had a weak identity at this point: with an increasingly conservative profile, it showed litle inclination to move toward reform, and acted against the interests of its traditional movement constituency. The SPD thus possessed poor efficacy as well: members of its supporting coalition defected when they perceived the party's program to be narrowly defined and contrary to their interests. The *Grünen* advanced where they addressed the leftist and environmental themes the SPD rejected, and that shaped their red/green identity afterward. In France, the PS addressed identity, and gained in efficacy. It represented strong movement toward change, and bridged ideological divisions between Left, New Left, and Center as it positioned itself as the main force of opposition to the Giscard regime of the 1970s, and later as the party in government. During this formative period, the first ecological lists in France benefited by emphasizing their political independence and autonomy from the Left and Right, as the *Verts* would do several years later. Where they advanced a left-ecological strategy similar to that of the West German Greens at the same point, the *Verts* failed to define themselves.

Prototypes in the Federal Republic of Germany

In West Germany, one social movement organization embodied the political diversity of the ecological movement in its earliest years. That was the *Bundesverband Bürgerinitiativen Umweltschutz* (BBU), created in 1972 as a political umbrella for the citizens' action groups that had sprung up in the previous few years.[1] When the *Bürgeriniativen* (BIs) first emerged in 1970, they were oriented toward local concerns of moderate middle-class citizens. The BIs then began to expand the scope of their agenda to focus on fundamental opposition to technology, on problems in infrastructure planning, and on the failures of the welfare state. The BBU's decision to compete with the established parties by fielding candidates in local and regional elections was particularly important in this political shift within the movement. At that point, left-wing activists began to appreciate the BBU's potential to oppose the governing class. Militants from the SPD Left, Jusos, and Communist splinter groups filtered in, bringing organizational and political expertise.[2]

In Hamburg, a left-ecological list grew from these diverse roots. A local BI federation, the Lower Elbe Citizens' Initiatives for Environmental Protection, supported a move to run candidates in the city-state elections of 1978. The resulting *Bunte List* (BL) was a left-leaning but heterogeneous coalition that included members of the BIs, ecologists, womens' groups, gay rights groups, as well as representatives of the trade unions and far Left *Kommunischer Bund* (KB).[3] In West Berlin, the *Alternative Liste* (AL), was formed in 1978 with a similar rainbow coloration, which, after a dispute, allowed activists from the Maoist *Kommuniste Partei Deutschland* (KPD) to participate. Conservative ecological slates also formed during this period.[4] Karl Beddermann, a CDU candidate in Lower Saxony, formed the *Umweltschutzpartei* (USP) in 1977. This organization aimed to oppose nuclear power from within the political system and excluded radicals who wanted deeper reform. In Schleswig-Holstein, a green list was led by a farmer named Baldur Springmann who had once been involved with the German radical Right.[5] A list that united several regional groups, the *Grüne Liste Schleswig–Holstein* (GLSH), stressed the primacy of ecology over social justice, and its statutes contained clauses against dual membership that would effectively exclude activists from leftist organizations. Herbert Gruhl, a right-wing conservationist and CDU dissident, helped form the *Grüne Aktion Zukunft* (Green Action Future, or GAZ) in Frankfurt during 1978. Gruhl's writings, which advanced authoritarian solutions for ecological problems, espoused conservative moral values, and rejected direct democracy, have often been cited as models of right-wing ecological thought.[6]

There were also centrist parties or lists that united moderate environmentalist elements with nondogmatic New Left currents. The *Aktionsgemeinschaft Unabhängiger Deutscher* (AUD), a minor party in the *Länder* since the 1960s, had sought a third way between capitalism and socialism and emphasized environmental over social questions. Unlike the right-wing ecological parties, though, the centrists were willing to work with leftists within a direct democratic format (which allowed leftist cadres to operate within the newer ecological organizations).[7] A similar alliance of moderate environmentalists and left-wing activists was to steer the *Grünen* when they first formed a unified national organization.

Prototypes in France

As in West Germany, early ecological lists in France tapped the energies of flourishing environmental and antinuclear movements with encouraging results. Yet, as was the case with the West German movement, ideological heterogeneity stood in the way of accord or coalition. The French antinuclear movement was troubled by antagonism between radical left-wing and environmentalist elements. The violent tactics of some left-wing groups at a protest in Malville in the Rhône-Alpes region incurred strong police action, causing one death. The effect was to lead moderates to look on the leftist cadres as opportunists otherwise weakly committed to the environmental cause. Further, the first ecological electoral lists were fairly heterogenous: *SOS-Environnement* was right of center, whereas *Écologie '78* was more *autogestionnaire*. One thing all the currents had in common was their aversion to organizing itself. This anarchist tendency spanned the French alternative Left and was a response to the extreme centralization of the French administration, party system, and nuclear power structure.[8] The *Réseaux des Amis de la Terre* (RAT) was the environmental movement's only national political structure before 1979. They, too, were oriented as much toward activity at the grassroots as toward national politics.[9] French ecologists thus favored running a series of "biodegradable" lists, dissolved after each election, which they used only to air their views.

Two national party organizations that did form toward the turn of the decade nevertheless had quite different views of the political strategy and type of organization the ecological movement should advance. The *Mouvement d'Écologie Politique* (MEP), which formed in 1979, favored a national structure run from a central bureau, and had a relatively conservative outlook.[10] Renegades from the MEP's founding conference created the *Confédération Écologiste* (CE) in June 1980. The CE stressed decentralization, and was animated by left-wing activists with an *autogestionnaire* background, such as Didier Anger and Yves Cochet. The RAT refused to participate in the negotiations between the two other forces, and withdrew from political action altogether in late 1982. It would take seven years of negotiations and false starts until a permanent, unified green party—*Les Verts*—formed from these heterogenous groups.

Cues from Left-Right Competition

No sooner was there momentum behind the formation of permanent parties than the ecologists began to experience the galvanizing impact of party system competition. The strength and ideological position of the socialist party was a key factor structuring the incentives and constraints for the ecologists. In the Federal Republic, the government and party elite of the SPD were moving toward the Center, precisely as German society was becoming more polarized between Right and Left.[11] The SPD's right turn between 1974 and 1980 alienated a broad segment of the party's electoral support.[12] Leftists were alienated by the SPD governments' tendency to take the side of law and order *vis-à-vis* the alternative Left and the militant cadre parties. Workers opposed cuts in their pensions. Environmental issues had strong resonance with mainstream voters, but here as well, the SPD seemed to act against their wishes. The Brandt administration's strategy of investment and growth after the oil crisis of 1973 meant a turn toward nuclear power. Schmidt continued this course, and also cut back on pollution control expenditures in 1975.[13] The time was ripe for a coalition rallying disaffected socialists and environmentalists.

The SPD's increasing tilt in the direction of growth and security correlates with successes for the left-leaning ecological lists in local and *Land* contests and poor scores for the right-wing ecological groups. The left-leaning BL placed better than the conservative groups in Hamburg in the city-state elections of 1978. The Hamburg branch of the centrist AUD received 0 percent (i.e., 591 votes), and the conservative *Grüne Liste Umwelt* won 1.0 percent, whereas the BL scored 3.5 percent. In West Berlin, the *Alternative Liste* (AL), which had a democratic socialist platform, won 3.7 percent in October 1978, despite negative publicity surrounding its inclusion of KPD members. In Hesse in the fall of 1978, Herbert Gruhl and the GAZ ran on a conservative platform to win only 0.9 percent.[14] In Schleswig-Holstein in 1979, the conservative GLSH won 2.4 percent of the vote. Later, in 1981, the radical AL beat a conservative *Grüne Berliner Liste* with 7.2 percent, vs. 0.3 percent, respectively. Even in conservative Bavaria, a GAZ/AUD alliance won only 1.8 percent.

A Green/Rainbow List in Bremen won the first major success for political ecology in Germany in the *Landtag* election of September 1979. It won 5.1 percent of the vote, clearing the numerical threshold for representation in the *Landtag*. Radical leftists from Bremen had united with centrist environmentalists behind a program of democratic and environmental reform. Their success made Bremen the model for the German Greens. It showed that a fusion of environmental and democratic socialist themes, wedded to a strategy of reform rather than revolution, could rally left-leaning and moderate voters.[15] A similar Left/Center alliance took control when the national *Grüne* party was formed the next year, thus defining the national party's identity for the next decade. When negotiations began to found a national ecological party in West Germany, there was a delicate balance between Left, Right, and Center. At a conference at Offenbach preparing for the founding of a permanent party in November 1979, the issue of dual membership was a particularly sore point. Conservatives strongly opposed any measure that would permit the leftists' incorporation into the new party. A compromise was reached in which members were required to join as individuals, not as organized groups, but would not be excluded for previous activities in the leftist cadres. This policy was sustained in later congresses by centrist leaders who, recognizing the success of the Bremen model, wanted to broaden the party's political base to span Left and Green.

While West Germany's leading center-left party lost ground, the French Socialist Party was on the rise. The rise of a strong center-left force in France, and the strategy of Left Union, meant that the French party system at the end of the 1970s was shaped no longer by the predominance of the Gaullists on the Right, but by more even and bipolar patterns of competition. With two poles evenly matched, the ecologists had more to gain by remaining unaligned than by identifying themselves with the Left portion of the political spectrum, as the West German ecologists did.[16] Thus early French ecological parties or lists took an approach that resembled the autonomous strategy of the Waechterian current in the *Verts* almost ten years later. In the campaign for the 1978 Legislative elections, *Écologie '78* and *SOS-Environnement* put aside their differences to form the *Collectif '78*. It was extremely loose in structure, officially nonaligned. Its sole aim was to exploit France's double-ballot electoral system and bipolar balance of party power to the greens' advantage. If the ecologists could win a significant number of votes on the first ballot, they could get publicity and force the leading parties to compete for the votes of their supporters on the second turn. *Collectif '78* won no seats, having run 221 candidates, with 4.8 percent of the vote where these candidates were present. Yet scores were between 10 percent and 18 percent in Paris, Normandie, Alsace, and the Rhône area (the *Verts* would continue to have strong showings in these regions throughout the 1980s and early 1990s). Further, they attained the goals they had set for themselves: to make local citizens aware of the problems in their communities, to get nationwide publicity for their ideas, and to force political parties—Right as much as Left—to promise action on environmental problems.[17]

After François Mitterrand acceded to the presidency in 1981, tactical alliances with the Left and Right were no longer viable. Due to the New Left credentials of the PS, the ecologists risked becoming politically engulfed by it. Simply endorsing the new government in the hope of winning reform follow was not an acceptable option either. Mitterrand's promises of a moratorium on nuclear power, a national referendum on the issue, and a research program for alternatives sources of energy never materialized after he took office.[18] Now in control of the Gaullist-designed nuclear defense structure, he became its apologist, and he was a staunch supporter of the NATO two-track decision. The French Right, associated with the repression of antinuclear protests under Giscard, hardly represented a haven for ecological opposition to the Mitterrand regime. The Socialist Party had the power to eclipse ecology in the political arena, and also to ignore its demands. Opposing it became the central strategic question for the French ecologists.

The early ecological lists did not meet this challenge. At that point, they had no real defining identity: they lacked an image of the overall direction of political action or social change that would set them apart from the party that came to power with the promise to "change life." They depended on the novelty of the environmental issue and the palpability of local environmental problems to attract votes.[19] In addition, they lacked an alternative program. Their program was largely negative: it centered on nonnegotiable demands to stop or slow nuclear construction. Similarly, the *Verts'* immediate precursors failed to offer anything that distinguished them from the PS or the alternative Left (which was also overshadowed by the PS's rise). A twelve-point program presented by *Aujourd'hui l'Écologie* during the 1981 presidential election had no reference specifically to the environment. Half of the materials were also mentioned in the PS's program.[20] Programs of the MEP and CE had placed far more emphasis on social themes such as unemployment.[21] The scores for these early lists indicate the weaknesses of the left-ecological strategy in France. In the March 1982 Cantonal elections, they scored only 0.4 percent. In the Municipals of March 1983—despite the electorate's rebuke of the PS at this critical juncture—the ecologists won 0.5 percent nationwide.

Disappointment with PS government may have had the positive effect of pushing the ecologists to unite in a permanent national organization.[22] In November 1983, the MEP and CE finally agreed to form *Les Verts / Confédération Ecologiste / Parti Écologiste*; they officially united at Clichy in January 1984. Yet the early *Vert* programs were also close to those of the Left during the same years. *Les Verts: Europe Écologie*, prepared for the 1984 European Parliament elections, emphasized social justice, and the rights of racially and socially excluded groups.[23] The *Verts* received 3.37 percent, though that was matched by Brice Lalonde's *Entente Radical Écologiste*, with 3.31 percent. Yet the *Verts* scores would dip once again to around 1 percent in the next elections, the 1986 Legislatives. Sainteny observes that the *Verts* lacked an alternative program at this point: the platforms cited here were neither coherent nor specific in their proposals.[24]

In light of these ambiguities in the French ecologists' strategy, it is impossible to conclude that one strategy or another was ever proven to fit the situation in France to the extent that it was in West Germany at this stage. A left-ecological strategy, however, clearly risked moving into occupied terrain. Where the PS combined identity and efficacy, the French Greens had to find some new means to define their own identity. While the *Verts* struggled over this question, the German Greens were beginning an astonishing political rise.

Chapter Seven

Defining Moments: Finding a Niche in the Party System

Defining Moments in West Germany: 1980–1983

After its recapture of the *Bundestag* in 1980, the SPD government of Helmut Schmidt was pulled to the Right by economic recession, and by its coalition partner, the FDP, further alienating the party's constituency. As tensions mounted, the FDP switched to form a government with Christian Democracts, and the SPD returned to parliamentary opposition status in 1982. The SPD's acts of undermining their own efficacy would continuously shape the Greens' identity. Left-wing activists gradually entered the newer party, and more and more SPD voters switched allegiances, some to the Greens and some to the CDU/CSU/FDP coalition.

Neither the SPD nor its Chancellor believed their policies ran against the long-run interests of their working-class constituents. The official position of the SPD at this point, and well afterward, was summarized in a polemic published in 1981 by political scientist Richard Löwenthal, a member of the SPD

Right. The article, entitled "Identität und Zukunft der SPD" ("Identity and Future of the SPD"), argued that there was a stark tradeoff between ecology and social democracy.[1] The interests of the working class, along with those of the middle class, lay in growth and stability. The West German protest culture and the ecology movement—both represented by the *Grünen*—stood opposed to those interests. Any move to try to cover the party's left flank by embracing postindustrial issues, then, would squander the sympathy of voters that Löwenthal saw as his party's "natural" base. This view ignored certain divisions in that base. By assuming that the middle class clearly stood in the Center, it elided cleavages between more elite or older professionals and younger new middle-class voters open to postindustrial themes. As we observed, the SPD's vacillating policy on NATO missiles in Germany would further strain its credibility with its more progressive supporters, and indeed with a wide section of the German public.

Ecologists' gains in the *Land* and city-state contests before 1980 had shown that a left-ecological identity had the greatest potential to advance the new politics. A majority of delegates to the formative conferences of the *Grüne* party appreciated that fact. At the party's founding conference at Karlsruhe in January 1980, the contentious issue of dual membership was left to the regional branches of the party (which tacitly favored the leftist militants who operated there). In addition, ecoconservatives like Gruhl and Springmann failed to prevent the inclusion of left-wing proposals in the draft of the *Federal Program*, produced at Saarbrucken in March of that year. Furthermore, the conservatives obtained no seats in the party's executive at a conference at Dortmund preparing the Greens for the 1980 campaign for the *Bundestag,* and an environmentalist/leftist alliance emerged to steer the party.[2] Gruhl and the conservatives then quit to form a new organization, the *Ökologisch-Demokratische Partei* (ÖDP), which obtained only marginal scores afterward. In more conservative or rural states, where the Greens themselves tended to be less radical, such as Bavaria, Rhineland-Palatinate, and Schleswig-Holstein, they did poorly.[3]

If the SPD's decline was playing into the *Grünen*'s hands, however, their success was not assured. That would depend on whether or not they had a viable strategy. In their first nationwide contest, the 1980 *Bundestag* elections, the *Grünen* felt a lurch in the momentum they had built up with *Land* victories in Bremen and Hamburg. With 1.5 percent, the new party fell short of clearing the 5 percent hurdle needed to send deputies to parliament. This setback may have been out of the Greens' control.[4] The SPD, with Schmidt at the helm, prevailed with 42.9 percent of the vote (a plurality needed to form the government), due in part to the unpopularity of the CDU/CSU chancellor candidate, flamboyant nationalist Franz Josef Strauss. Potential supporters for the Greens may have chosen the SPD to block Strauss's chances.[5] Yet the problems may also be linked to the *Grünen's* own efforts to define themselves. The *1980 Federal Program* contained many statements of left-ecological principles, but few practical measures. The program constitutes a cluster of demands appended by discrete groups, not a coherent set of prescriptions for change.[6] That may have given marginal voters few clues as to what the party would do if it was given the chance to influence policy at the national level. The *Grünen*, in other words, did not combine the two components of an effective ecological strategy at this point. They had a defining identity, but not an alternative program. The 1980 *Bundestag* elections did show signs of the promise the future held for the *Grünen* and their left-ecological identity. 28.6 percent of voters who chose the Greens on the first ballot split their tickets, choosing the SPD on the second.[7] More and more new middle-class voters defected from the SPD to the Greens.[8] The Greens also began to take votes from the FDP, whom they would eventually supplant as the champions of civil and political rights within the German political system. Rallying portions of the electoral Center as well as the Left, the new party grew in efficacy.

Land and city-state contests in the interim between the 1980 and 1983 *Bundestag* elections also tested the viability of the *Grünen's* strategy *vis-à-vis* the SPD. In June 1982, when the green organization in Hamburg won 7.9 percent, prospects for a red/green coalition emerged for the first time (the only other option, a grand coalition with the SPD and CDU, was not politically feasible). The radical *Grüne Alternative Liste* (GAL), formed in March 1982 out of remnants of the leftist cadres and the BL. After the elections, the GAL developed the notion of "tolerance" of an SPD government, which permitted support for individual bills sponsored by the SPD legislation, without formal participation in or endorsement of the SPD. Yet they demanded some stiff concessions in return: emergency unemployment measures, an immediate end to the government's austerity program, and an immediate withdrawal from nuclear power. Despite pressure from within his own party to reject any accommodation to the Greens' demands, Mayor Klaus Von Dohnanyi responded by alluding to the significant areas of common ground between the local SPD and the Greens on aspects of environmental protection and labor market policy. When the Greens remained adamant about their proposals, Von Dohnanyi called new elections, in which the SPD won an absolute majority without the greens, whose score fell by some two thousand votes to 6.8 percent. The GAL had stressed identity over efficacy—but they failed to establish a defining identity *vis-à-vis* their competitor. They assumed that their strict adherence to their maximal demands would heighten public awareness of their issues. Thus they stonewalled while Von Dohnanyi captured red/green territory, making it his own. The Hamburg Greens let him define them as members of a radical fringe.The mayor's encroachment on moderate green territory was also aided by the GAL's utter lack of an alternative program. That was precisely what the GAL wanted to avoid: they believed proposing concrete practical measures amounted to a dangerous drift into incrementalism and compromise.[9]

An election in the state of Hesse during the same year also yielded a red/green numerical majority, though no coalition formed immediately there either. Relations between the Greens and Social Democrats in Hesse were at first only marginally more favorable than those in Hamburg. Prospective minister-president Holger Börner, a former construction worker with a reactionary outlook, was initially a staunch supporter of the SPD Right's position barring cooperation with the Greens. After the Greens' refusal to pass the state budget, Börner called new elections in September 1983, asking the voters for an absolute majority. Taking note of their support for green issues, however, Börner campaigned on promises of an environmental business and jobs program (which was actually first proposed by the Greens). The Green's score in September 1983 fell from 8 percent to 5.9. Their loss stemmed in part from the dissipation of popular antagonism toward local airport and nuclear construction projects, from which the Greens had benefited earlier. Yet the SPD's sudden embrace of their issue was also a factor.[10] Börner, though conservative, had undermined the Hessian Greens' defining identity by incorporating green issues into his party's program. Further, the Greens were unable to develop an alternative program in the short time they had to prepare for the new elections.

Setbacks in these state contests indicated that the *Grünen* had not yet developed their left-ecological identity into a clear overall strategy. The opposite was the case in national elections in 1983. The state of the West German economy made it urgent that the *Grünen* expand the socioeconomic portion of their agenda for the campaign. In a country where full employment had long been a goal, unemployment now touched 2.5 million lives, and all of the parties advanced their own proposals to address it. Meeting first at Hagen in November 1982, then at Sindelfingen in January 1983, the Greens tried to improve the *1980 Federal Program* in the matter of concrete proposals. The thirty-nine-page program developed the socialist and ecological themes we examined in chapter 5. It advocated more decentralized, democratized workplaces, ecological forms of investment, and major training programs for unemployed youths.[11] It appealed for support from grassroots social movements and the left wing of the trade unions. Further, the Sindelfingen draft laid out certain concrete steps toward change, such as work sharing and a new middle-class/trade union alliance. By 1983, then, the Greens had arrived at the alternative program they lacked earlier. The *Grünen*'s left-ecological identity, first articulated at Saarbrucken in 1980 and developed at Sindelfingen in 1983, had posed an alternative to both the Keynesianism of *Modell Deutschland* and the neoliberalism of the incoming Kohl government. The German Greens had advanced a positive mobilizing vision that the other parties had either ceded or lacked. With 5.6 percent of the vote, the *Grünen* sent twenty-seven delegates to the *Bundestag*. Meanwhile, the SPD suffered defections to the bourgeois parties (1.6 million votes) and to the Greens (750,000), holding only 38.2 percent.

Defining Moments in France: 1984–1988

In 1984, just after the German Greens had entered the *Bundestag*, the *Verts* had nowhere to go but up. As we noted in chapter 4, two main strategic tendencies coexisted within the tiny, newly formed party. Each had its own views as to how to rescue French political ecology from its poor scores. Yves Cochet wanted to define ecology's identity within the Left of the party system. Antoine Waechter sought an independent position instead. In certain respects, the period between 1984 and 1988 might have been an auspicious moment for Cochet's version. As in West Germany a few years before, a Socialist government had shifted from the Left to the Center—albeit in a far more abrupt and dramatic manner. In 1982, the PS government had begun a policy of monetary discipline and fiscal austerity. In 1984, a new, more technocratic government was installed, and its moves to restructure strategic French industries brought workers to the street. Antidemocratic tendencies were manifest in the style as well as the substance of Socialist governance. Nationalizations and reforms in industrial relations proposed in the *Projet Socialiste* had been introduced by fiat, without consultation with the parties affected.[12] Further, the PS had continued to fare poorly in environmental matters. In the Rainbow Warrior Affair of 1985, French secret service divers sank a Greenpeace ship protesting nuclear tests in New Zealand with the presumed support of the Defense Ministry.

If trends in 1984 seem to have favored the emergence of an Alternative Left party, the decline of the actual parties of the Left—the PSU, the Communists, and other small independent Left parties, such as the FGA and LCR—did not bode well. The decline of these forces to the Left of the Socialist Party has to be explained in part by the resilience of the PS itself. The Socialists lost seats in by-elections in 1982, and then lost the mayoralties of fifteen large towns in the Municipals of March 1983. They also lost their majority in the French National assembly in 1986. In this case, however, due to Mitterrand's institution of a proportional representation ballot system, they cut their losses to 32 percent (the emergence of the National Front helped: it held the neo-Gaullist/liberal bloc's mandate at 43 percent). Further, Mitterrand's reelection to the presidency in 1988 meant that the Socialists would return to form the government once again.

In spite of its neoliberal turn, the PS still attracted working-class voters in the 1986 legislatives and the 1988 presidentials fleeing the PCF's self-inflicted decline. The PS also sustained a positive image in the eyes of new middle-class voters.[13] Bereft of the left-leaning economic programmatic themes that defined them when they first took power, the PS and Mitterrand turned toward civil liberties as an alternative. The underlying aim was to legitimize, post hoc, their turn to economic liberalism, since the defense of personal liberties was portrayed as a desirable parallel to the opening of private economic initiatives.[14] The law-and-order platform of the right-wing government, and the policies of Interior Minister Charles Pasqua, helped the PS define itself all the more clearly as the defender of individual liberties. In 1988, the PS supported strengthening judicial rights and an end to the death penalty.[15]

As the *Verts'* first annual *Assemblée Générale* met at Dijon in November 1984, the technocratic, neoliberal turn of the PS had just been formalized with a change of government the preceding July. The left-ecological leaders' response was a program of radical socioeconomic reform—that is, one founded on the same principles and concerns as those issued by the *Grünen* at Sindelfingen the year before. Typically, the left-ecologists emphasized the economic over the ecological. Anger proposed to "give the economy the first place in our operations," in order to oppose the notion of neoliberalism's inevitability.[16] At a congress at Lille in 1985, Cochet argued that it was important that political ecology show its competency in a range of policy issues, such as social security, international trade, and new technologies.[17] Though the list of possible allies was subject to change, it would at times include the Maoist LCR, the Trotskyist FGA, the PSU, along with feminists and advocates of the rights of *beurs* (young first-generation natives of Arab descent).[18] Perhaps the most closely watched effort to construct a new force for opposition to the regime was the *Arc-en-ciel* movement of late 1986 and 1987. Inspired by the *Verts'* calls for convergence of the independent Left, and organized by an antiracist group, "SOS-Racisme," the *Arc-en-ciel* movement once more tried to rally new social movement and New Left forces: "self-management activists, feminist environmentalists, regionalists, third world activists, trade unions, neighborhood associations, anti-racist, non-violent and antinuclear movements."[19]

With their left-ecological profile, the *Verts* lacked a defining identity. The Socialist government had already retreated on its radical proposals to redress socioeconomic justice, and the burden was on the *Verts* to show what set them apart from the other organizations to the Left of the PS and the programs associated with them.[20] The problems were reflected in the marginal scores ecology received at this time. As we noted, the European Parliament elections of 1984 saw 3.37 percent of the vote go to the *Verts* (though the ecological vote was split by a rival list led by Lalonde, which won 3.31 percent). In the Cantonal elections of 1985, the *Verts* scored .79 percent nationwide, with 4.8 percent where an ecologist was present. In the Legislative elections of March 1986, the *Verts* won 1.2 percent overall, and 2.74 percent where an ecological candidate was present—and that despite the windfall for a small party stemming from the institution of proportional representation. The Regionals of the same month, also following proportional representation, brought the *Verts* 2.4 percent of the vote. They did win three seats on regional councils in regions where the environmental and antinuclear movement had been strong. Even here, though, there were setbacks: the numbers were lower by 5.5 percent in the Manche (Normandy), 5.7 percent in Bas-Rhin (Alsace), and 6.5 percent in Haut-Rhin (Alsace) than the previous score in the respective regions.

Since they had delivered such poor results, the left-ecological leadership of the *Verts* faced a challenge from within at the next *Assemblée Générale*, which was held in Paris in November 1986.[21] The challenge was led by the pure ecologists, whose winning motion bore the heading "fundamentalist," and aimed for the "unyielding affirmation of the originality and identity of ecology."[22] The pure ecological insurgents rejected any type of coalition in principle, but they focused most of their energy, however, on stopping coalition with left-wing parties. While acknowledging some "convergence in analysis," with New Left organizations like the PSU or the FGA, they held that "a profound difference in our core aspirations renders any union impossible, since that would deny the identity of one of the partners."[23] Coalition, in their view, was no solution to the *Verts'* weakness, since prospective allies among the Extraparliamentary Left were weak themselves. The pure ecologists also believed that the socialists could afford to ignore their demands in the event of an alliance, whereas the ecologists' independence would automatically suffer.[24] In a meeting of over six hundred militants from all over France—large for that time— the pure ecological line prevailed 413 to 196.

Two of the new spokespersons, Waechter and Andrée Buchmann, were already serving in municipal councils in Alsace, and had close ties with environmentalist organizations there and in other regions of France.[25] Waechter was particularly effective at communicating with the average militant, far more than leftists like Cochet. Like Waechter, most of the youthful militants had their formative experiences working in the grassroots environmental groups, not in political parties. And like Waechter, they were highly demoralized by ecology's poor showings in elections, even if they remained dedicated to it.[26] Waechter, then, advanced a strategy of identity: he saw the environmental movement as the bedrock of the ecology party.

He outlined the ways the party would be built on the movement in an interview shortly after his current won the majority at the *Assemblée Generale*.[27] To enter Parliament, Waechter argued, the Greens had to strive for better representation at the grassroots first. They should try to "create a dynamic" in the Cantonal elections of summer 1988 by winning a modest share of votes and gaining publicity. For the next contest, the 1989 Municipals, Waechter wanted to multiply the party's 1983 score by ten: that is, from three hundred to three thousand. This figure was far larger than the number of candidates the party itself, with only about one thousand members, could muster. Thus the *Verts* were counting on the support of independent environmental activists with proven stature in each locality. The results of the 1989 municipals, with 8.1 percent of the vote, and 1,369 Green candidates elected, fell short of Waechter's goals. Yet strong showings in Alsace and Brittany, for example, indicated that the existence of local environmental problems had expanded public awareness of the *Verts'* key issues.[28]

Emphasis on the environmental movement also benefitted Waechter's campaign for the presidency in 1988. A pamphlet for the campaign, *Les Verts et la nature*, alluded solely to problems of the physical environment: damage to the water supply, to the ozone layer, and climate change; plus related issues such as wilderness preservation and hunting.[29] For the first time, the new party had truly defined their identity around the environment, the one issue that set it apart from the mainstream parties, all of whom had poor environmental records. The *Verts* also had an alternative program: *Les Verts et la nature* called for numerous concrete measures to protect the environment, such as the creation of special environmental agencies, decentralization of authority over environmental policy to the regions, and freer access to public information about the environment. Waechter's presidential run brought 3.78 percent of the vote on the first ballot, a little less than the score for Brice Lalonde's in 1981. These results, while modest, brought the *Verts* other gains, and that confirmed and strengthened their pure ecological direction. Waechter's score was high enough to qualify his party for public funds to cover campaign expenses, which were turned over to create new staff and prepare for the municipal campaign coming the next year.[30] Membership doubled during this period—that is, from around one thousand to two thousand between the April election and November of 1988.[31] Above all, Waechter's score in the 1988 presidential contest brought favorable publicity. Waechter unexpectedly outperformed the highly regarded Pierre Juquin, a former spokesperson for the PCF.[32] Juquin's campaign bore the rubric "A Red and Green Alternative" and his candidacy was sponsored by some of the same organizations that had been courted by the left-ecologists in the *Verts*. As it turned out, Juquin scored only 2.1 percent, with 639,000 votes, whereas Waechter rallied 1,115,000 French voters.

The essence of the pure ecological strategy Waechter represented was to marginalize socioeconomic themes associated with a still-powerful Left. Juquin's strategy did the opposite, since he still supported state intervention and other policies once favored by the PS. The German-style fusion of Red and Green had failed once again in France. The environmental movement served as the most viable symbol of the aspirations of citizens then increasingly alienated by a closed state administration and the PS's comfortable proximity to power. At this defining moment in their evolution, the *Grüne* and *Vert* branches parted off from the trunk of the worldwide ecology movement.

Chapter Eight

Consolidation—and New Tensions

Consolidation in West Germany: 1983–1989

Despite the *Grünen*'s advances in the state parliaments, and their success in the 1983 Bundestag elections, the SPD still did not respond to the challenge. Although a cohort of new leaders was beginning to lead the SPD in the *Länder*, the next chancellor candidate, Johannes Rau, a conservative, continued to reject the idea of courting the younger, left-leaning segment of the SPD electorate by addressing the new politics. That in turn gave the Greens little reason to change their strategy of integrating left-wing or socialist demands with green themes. Still, some the Greens' very successes began to expose the latent strains within the party.

Land and city-state elections brought many further opportunities for alliances between the Greens and the SPD during this period. Where the *Grünen* faced a conservative SPD leader, they fared well. As we saw in the last chapter, the elections in Hesse of September 1983 failed to produce an absolute majority for the SPD, and negotiations thus continued on a red/green accord and state budget. A formal coalition agreement was finally reached in

October 1985, but it collapsed in February 1987 after a dispute over nuclear power. Joschka Fischer, the Environment Minister in Hesse, had demanded the phasing out of two nuclear power plants. Fischer resigned when Börner struck a tacit deal with the conservative government in Bonn to maintain the plants. The outcome of the coalition experiment led the voters to scuttle the idea of renewing the SPD/Green coalition in the elections that followed in April 1987.[1] They punished the SPD particularly harshly: its score fell by six points, to only 40.2 percent, and thus it no longer controlled Hesse. Yet despite the failure of the coalition experiment, voters actually rewarded the Hessian Greens, whose score rose from 5.9 to 9.4 percent.

That outcome fits our hypotheses. The green party preserved its defining identity, posing a clear alternative to the socialist party (which they had failed to accomplish in the last Hessian elections of September 1983). Börner was not a green-minded, youthful modernizer but a member of the SPD old guard who had only accepted the idea of a coalition after realizing he had no other choice. Even moderates like Fischer could appear uncompromising next to him. Fischer thus held fast to one of the pillars of the party's core demands, an exit from nuclear energy. Furthermore, before the nuclear plant debacle, the Greens had not only outlined but helped enact an alternative program. Their rise put pressure on SPD to propose its "ecologically oriented business and jobs program" for the 1983 election. In budget negotiations afterward, the Hessian Greens helped pass a series of environmental and social reform laws, including measures to create jobs in environmental industries.[2]

Where the Greens faced the younger SPD modernizers, however, they had far more difficulties defining their identity.[3] The Greens in the Saarland, like their Hessian counterparts, had an alternative program that was designed to rally working-class support in what was one of Germany's most concentrated and by then depressed regions of heavy industry. Yet the Saarland Greens faced an SPD candidate who was more progressive than Börner, Oskar Lafontaine. Lafontaine was quite effective in bridging working-class and progressive new middle-class concerns. After promising polls, the Greens went down to defeat in March 1985, gaining only 2.5 percent of the vote. In 1990, Lafontaine won an absolute majority again, and the SPD continues to govern alone.

In North Rhine-Westphalia, the Greens had similar problems developing a defining identity. These did not stem from the characteristics of the SPD candidate, as was the case in the Saarland. The Premiership in North Rhine-Westphalia was held by Johannes Rau, like Börner a member of the party's Right. That should have meant that a moderate left-ecological position was a viable one for the Greens. Further, as in the Saarland and Hesse, the Greens had tried to develop an alternative program that could draw disaffected working-class sectors away from the ruling party. Yet the Greens in North Rhine-Westphalia failed to convey the essence of their platform in a clear outward message. A compromise program that emerged after some difficult negotiations among party factions was too long and complex. The highly visible internal feuds clouded any sense of the Greens' common purpose in the eyes of voters. The NRW Greens thus failed not only to define their identity *vis-à-vis* the socialist party, but to convey a clear identity of any kind (that outcome ought to have sent sobering signals to the national *Grüne* party organization). Despite high expectations, the NRW Greens met with defeat in the March 1984 elections, winning only 4.6 percent.[4]

Hamburg Greens had the opposite problem. As we noted in the last chapter, they placed strong, perhaps too much, emphasis on identity, with no attention to program or policy at all. They had aimed to drive a wedge between factions in the SPD and profit from an ensuing crisis. If they took a radical proenvironmental stance on every issue, they could force the SPD left wing to lean toward its greener side, and exacerbate the natural lines of division between this group and the party's proemployment Right.[5] In 1986, the Hamburg Greens managed an impressive 10.4 percent. Yet they declined later, in May 1987, to just below 7 percent. In a tactical move, Von Dohnanyi had called new elections after he discovered that it was simply impossible to find common programmatic ground with the Greens. Von Dohnanyi's explicit aim was to renegotiate the SPD/Green alliance. But his ploy had really been to paint the Green fundamentalists as recalcitrant and obstructionist, and it was apparently successful.

Similar patterns held in Lower Saxony in June 1986, where the Green's excessive focus on identity dashed high expectations. The SPD candidate for minister-president was Gerhard Schröder, a modernizer with a charismatic personality. Realists in Lower Saxony were positive about the prospects for a red/green coalition. Yet the nuclear accident at Chernobyl in the former Soviet Union occurred at this time, and Lower Saxon fundis, believing the catastrophe would automatically shift public opinion in their favor, renewed their call for an immediate exit from nuclear power. The effect was to make the election a referendum on Chernobyl, but as polls showed, the voters were less moved by the accident than party militants. The *Grünen* in Lower Saxony also suffered from associations made in the press (spurious, it turned out) with antinuclear protesters who had used violent tactics. For his part, Schröder skillfully avoided being painted into a pronuclear corner by offering to consider a phaseout of nuclear power in his home state if elected (this diverged from official SPD policy at that time). In sum, the Greens in Lower Saxony lacked an alternative program: they had only negative demands based on a single issue. *Vis-à-vis* the environment-conscious Schröder, they had a poor defining identity as well.[6] The SPD gained 5 points, scoring 42.1 percent, though the CDU/FDP prevailed, forming the government with a majority of only one seat.

City-state elections in Bremen, like Hesse, saw positive electoral scores for the Greens juxtaposed with failures in effecting a red/green coalition government. In September 1987, even a 10.2 percent score was judged a disappointment, since the SPD won an absolute majority and continued to govern alone. The Bremen Greens' score, though significant, was also a relative decline *vis-à-vis* their Bundestag votes in Bremen earlier that year, which totalled 14.5 percent. Still, compared to their last score in the city-state elections, the 1987 results were positive ones. The Bremen Greens' Center-Left strategy may have distinguished them from a rather conservative local SPD branch (many Greens in Bremen were defectors from its left-wing minority). The Bremen Greens won 11.4 percent in 1991, dislodging the SPD from its absolute majority there, and the two joined the FDP in what turned out to be a tense coalition. An SPD/CDU coalition took over in 1995, but the Greens raised their score to 13 percent.

The coalition experiment in the *Länder*, especially the one in Hesse, threw the national *Grüne* party into a state of crisis, since it aggravated the conflict between realists and fundamentalists surrounding the question of alliances and the Greens' possible adaptation to the political system. The realist position eventually prevailed when fundamentalists began to leave the party. But the fundamentalists had a point: the Greens' identity was indeed in danger. With a newer, younger leadership, and with the tacit blessing of their coalition partners, the SPD was encroaching on environmental territory in the *Länder*, and that process continued, slowly but surely, in the national party.

The *Grünen* did well in Federal elections when the SPD adopted a conservative strategy—and when they themselves remained united. Unlike many SPD leaders in the *Länder*, chancellor candidate Johannes Rau believed that his party should go it alone in its bid to regain control of the Bundestag in 1987. He asked the electorate to give the SPD an absolute majority and ruled out the possibility of a SPD/*Grüne* coalition in advance. Once again, Rau focused on traditional working-class economic concerns, with a view toward capturing the Center from the CDU/CSU/Liberal coalition.

The older party's rejection of the red/green coalition allowed the Greens to avoid addressing that thorny and divisive question themselves. Party spokesperson Antje Vollmer helped by fostering a rare degree of internal unity. Before other campaign work began, she managed to push through a compromise statement, in which the Greens would defer discussion of coalition strategy until after the elections. The truce in factional warfare left a breathing space for the *Grünen* to work on broadening their alternative program. While they reiterated earlier issues, such as opposition to nuclear energy and measures to check unemployment, they also added new ones, such as calls for Germany to leave NATO. Even more politically effective was the introduction of various proposals for women's rights, an issue with immense popular appeal, yet relatively underregarded by mainstream parties.

The 1987 elections to the Bundestag saw the German Greens' highest national score thus far: 8.7 percent. In this victory, their left-ecological programmatic work and left-wing party system identity bore their fullest fruit. Once more, the *Grünen* exploited the opportunity created by SPD's defensive conservatism. The SPD had clearly chosen to represent the establishment, leaving the Greens effectively as the only force of opposition demands at the national level. In 1987, the *Grüne* program offered left-leaning German voters a clear choice. After that point, as the *Grünen* fought over what to do with success, the SPD would succeed in blurring that choice.

Consolidation and New Tensions:
France 1988–1992

After Antoine Waechter's success in the presidential contest of 1988, the *Verts* continued to project a pure ecological identity. The principle of autonomy from the Left proved to be a valuable resource. By reversing the party's poor electoral scores, the left-ecological minority began to accept it, and the principles behind it were formalized at party congresses in the next several years. In contrast to the German Greens during the period just discussed, the strategy of the fundamentalists (i.e., Waechterians) became the strategy of the party—to such an extent that there was strong resistance toward making any tactical adjustments to changing political circumstances.

There was little in the actions or in the fortunes of the PS to change this position in favor of alliance or coalition. Taking note of the *Verts'* rising scores, the Socialist Party and its leader had begun to acknowledge the political potency of environmentalism, and to try to bring its leaders back into the orbit of the PS. Brice Lalonde became Secretary for the Environment, and later Minister. Mitterrand also asked Lalonde to form a party that would support the PS in the future; hence *Génération Écologie* was formed in May 1990. These types of friendly gestures had been made to the Communists and the PSU, and the *Verts* were not inclined to share their fate.[7] Further, despite Mitterrand's reelection in 1988, the PS's own weaknesses began to come to the surface— that is, ideological exhaustion, scandals, and factional infighting. Socialist decline, of course, created no more incentive for the *Verts* to change their strategy than Socialist overtures.

As we saw in the last chapter, the Municipal elections of March 1989 marked a turning point for ecological politics in France. In the European Parliament elections that followed that June, the *Verts* proved that they could perform well in an election where the political stakes and issues ranged beyond local problems. In the pamphlet for that campaign, *Les Verts et l'Europe,* the *Verts* developed the direct democratic and participatory themes around which the Waechterians had begun to redefine French ecology. Left-ecologist Yves Cochet supervised its publication; he now apparently accepted the centrality of the environment in the *Verts'* programmatic agenda. The 1989 European elections brought the *Verts'* highest independent score to date: 10.6 percent. The *Verts'* progressed at PS's expense.[8] The PS list led by Laurent Fabius won only 23.6 percent, close to their low point of 21 percent in 1984, during the protests against the first austerity program.

After these successes, militants approved the autonomy line at subsequent national party congresses. At the *Assemblée Générale* in Strasbourg in November of 1990, there were several motions passed which formalized the Waechterian strategy of nonalignment. One stipulated that the *Verts* reject all electoral agreements in which they would stand down in the second electoral ballot for a candidate who was better positioned to win. Another stated that where the *Verts* were unable to remain in the second round, they would refuse to give advice to their voters as to which candidate to support. A third motion, similar to that adopted by the *Grünen* in a concession to conservatives, prevented the possible influence of leftist groups from within the *Verts'* party organization. Statutes written at an earlier congress were revised to forbid double membership and to require members to join on an individual rather than group basis.

Certain implications in the autonomy strategy incited factional conflict at Strasbourg and at later congresses. The *Verts* official policy, and the controversy surrounding it, would damage their otherwise high levels of sympathy. At issue was the party's attitude toward France's extreme right-wing party, the Front National (FN). Would the *Verts'* principle of strict autonomy imply that its candidates should refuse to withdraw in the second round, even if doing so would help elect a well-placed FN candidate (that is, by weakening a candidate of any other party that might have placed first)? In the event that the *Verts* could not remain for the second round, would they refuse to advise their voters, even given the presence of a competitive FN candidate?

Once again, Waechter and Cochet led opposing camps. Waechter's reasoning conformed to logic of the identity strategy: the political system is uniformly corrupt, and change must be made at the roots, in civil society and in individual consciousness. A Waechterian strategic motion argued that

> to enter into a Republican Front or into a system of alliances against Le Pen is to admit that what separates us from other forces is less than what separates us from Le Pen; and that is to forget that it is these political forces that paved the way for Le Pen; it is also to make Le Pen appear credible [i.e., to his own supporters] when he says "there is only me and the others."[9]

The Waechterians believed that xenophobia had to be countered by education and assimiliation, not by the cynical rhetoric of the political class.They also argued that their voters could be trusted to avoid supporting an FN candidate without having to be told.

Cochet and other leftists (including Voynet) countered that it was precisely the system of republican institutions that was in danger and had to be defended. Even if the FN had a right to exist in principle, like any other organization in a democracy, its fundamental commitment to democracy itself was in doubt:

> The FN, even if it participates in elections, is an anti-republican, anti-democratic party, implicated in the history of European Fascism . . . which, if it found its power and its influence enhanced by the election of its candidates, might employ more forceful methods to achieve its aims.[10]

Once again, Waechter's argument prevailed over that of Cochet and his supporters. In a party committed to solidarity with the third world, cultural tolerance, and immigrants' rights, it is hard to conclude this result is a sign of racism or neofascist sympathies. Rather, it is an indication of militants' disgust with all of the leading parties, their deep-seated fear that Cochet would sell out ecology to the PS, and, above all, their satisfaction with the proven results of the autonomy strategy.[11]

In light of the momentum behind the principle of autonomy, it was approved once again at the *Assemblée Générale* at St-Brieuc in November 1991. The Greens were likely to score well in the upcoming elections to the Regional Councils, and they were willing to participate in choosing Regional Executives (these are voted in by Regional councillors once they are elected). Still, these were predicated on the prospective partner's acceptance of several nonnegotiable demands. These included the right to vote for immigrants in local elections, a phaseout of nuclear power within ten years, a moratorium on autoroute construction, an end to nuclear testing in the South Pacific, the institution of full proportional representation in French elections, and the institution of national referenda by popular initiative (rather than solely that of elected officials).[12]

St-Brieuc saw a slight modification of the earlier position adopted at Strasbourg toward the FN. The *Verts* would not vote for any Regional Council president if National Front votes were cast in his or her support. Any moderation in the *Verts'* policy regarding the National Front, however, had come too late. Positions outlined at Strasbourg the year before handed ready-made material to commentators in the press and in other parties inclined to see ecology as something inherently authoritarian, perhaps a Gothic export from across the Rhine. If the *Verts* had not already done enough to feed these perceptions and accusations, an incident brought on by former spokesperson Jean Brière fanned the flames. In April 1991, shortly after the start of the Persian Gulf War, Brière submitted a text to the *Conseil National Inter-Régionale* (CNIR), the *Verts'* internal parliament, identfying the "war-breeding" nature of Israel and the "Zionist lobby" as an incitement to the conflict.[13] A CNIR member Maryse Arditi, whose background is Jewish, made the statement public in a press meeting, in the hope of shocking the *Verts* out of complacency on the matter. While denouncing Brière's views, many activists still professed their belief that he had a right to enunciate them. Once again, the *Verts'* penchant for finding nuances in an ethically thorny matter became fodder for distortion and sensationalism in the press.[14]

Still more damaging was the fact that the *Verts'* apparent complacency with regard to extreme right-wing politics seemed to be mixed with suspicion of left-wing influences. Real trends were giving paranoia plenty to feed on. One by one, left-wing activists were deserting other organizations to join the ecology party.[15] In August 1991, Pierre Juquin—the Communist *rénovateur* and 1988 presidential hopeful whose numbers in that contest had paled next to Waechter's—made a request to join the *Verts* as an individual member. Juquin thus touched off the most aggravated and public instance of this paranoia. Waechterians feared that Juquin would be a natural leader for a left-ecological challenge to their majority.[16] Ironically, some members of the press saw Juquin's eventual admission as proof that the *Verts* were really an organization of the far Left, rather than of the far Right—and that muddled still further the distinctive political identity that they had fought to project.[17]

Most critically, ambiguities surrounding the *Verts*' autonomy strategy played into the hands of a more pragmatic challenger, *Génération Écologie*. The Waechterians' rigid adherence to the autonomy strategy allowed Lalonde to portray himself and his new organization as a foil for all that seemed to be amiss in the *Verts*. The results of the first turn of the March 1992 Regional Council elections revealed the problems abruptly. The scores for *GE* and the *Verts* were extremely close: 7.1 percent vs. 6.8 percent, respectively. Yet the *Verts* had lost over four percentage points since the last nationwide contest, the 1989 European Parliament elections. Further, they suffered in former regional strongholds. Lalonde is a native of Paris and quite well known there, and the *Verts* fell far behind GE (i.e., 6.9 percent to GE's 10.88 percent). Yet the *Verts* also declined in Alsace. Antoine Waechter and Andrée Buchmann, leaders of the pure ecological current, were incumbent Regional Councillors. They saw the *Verts*' local scores for the 1989 European elections chopped nearly in half (i.e., from 20.48 percent to 12.57 percent, whereas GE won 6.7 percent).

Analysis of GE's electorate in the March 1992 Regionals suggests that the newer party's moderate position on environmental reform had resonance with some of the *Verts*' potential voters. Many who were sympathetic to environmentalism now felt that they were closer in outlook to GE than the *Verts*.[18] GE picked up a few former *Vert* supporters, some 25 percent.[19] Like the *Verts* before it, GE also attracted Socialist votes, along with those of the centrist parties as well.[20] GE voters in 1992 tended to have higher salary levels than the *Verts*' electors, and were more politically moderate.[21] As we shall see, Lalonde's and GE's triumph did not last.

Chapter Nine

Cataclysm and Renewal

Two Cataclysmic Elections

To the astonishment of many observers, French and German ecology parties fell far short of expectations in parliamentary elections during the first years of the 1990s. Counter to indications in the polls, the *Grünen*, with only 4.8 percent, failed to reach the 5 percent threshold required for representation in the first all-German Bundestag elections of December of 1990. Also confounding the polls were the results for a unified ecological bloc, the *Entente Écologiste*, which received 7.7 percent and no seats in the French elections to the National Assembly of March 1993. The poor results would strain the ecology parties in each country to the point where key activists either quit or broke off to form new parties (that in turn paved the way for fundamental changes in the portion of the organizations that remained).

A comparison of the events that shook the German and French party systems in these elections might seem intractable. The first *Bundestag* elections in a newly unified Federal Republic were directly preceded by transnational social movements, complete regime changes, and diplomatic negotiations, and they had

115

truly international significance. French Legislative elections were more domestic in scope. The *Bundestag* elections were a major step in the unification of two previously divided societies, and of many political parties within them. Events in France involved more familiar actors and issues, though the ruling parties changed. In Germany, the SPD and the Greens were caught off guard by the momentum of unification and politically outstripped by the skill and timing of the right-wing leader, Helmut Kohl. In France, the Socialist Party, in power for twelve years, was more fully responsible for the outcome.

Nevertheless, the greens in each country had one thing in common: the limits of each party's strategy became clear. The *Grünen*'s left-ecological identity no longer distinguished them from a younger, greener SPD. The notion of ecology's special independence and urgency, pioneered by the *Verts* and embraced by GE, meant they lacked credibility when they tried to advance other issues like unemployment (the *Verts*' identity problem was compounded by an alliance with the mercurial Lalonde). In addition, both the SPD and PS made tactical advances into environmentalist territory and other postindustrial themes in the campaigns for these elections. Yet both socialist parties had severe setbacks, and the ecologists' identification with them may have affected their scores.

The Cataclysm: Germany

The conventional explanation for the *Grünen*'s poor performance in December 1990 centers on their critical position regarding the newly unified Federal Republic. Like the SPD, the *Grünen* warned of the immense financial cost and rapid pace of unification, and tended to regard the division of Germany as a stay against German aggression.[1] But this does not explain the defections by the *Grünen*'s former voters in the West. It seems doubtful that the Greens' typical voters would be motivated entirely by the nationalist fervor. Further, if the vote was also a sanction against the SPD on the unification issue, why was it that most of the Greens' defectors shifted to the SPD? Factional conflict may also have played a role in the *Grünen*'s poor showing in the 1990 Bundestag elections. The spectacle of intraparty feuds between fundis and realos reached a crisis point in the year or so before these elections, leaving the public to wonder whether they were a radical antisystem party or a reformist junior partner to the SPD.

Changes in the SPD at that time made the Greens' dilemma over the coalition question still more exquisite. A new cohort of leaders had finally incorporated environmentalist themes in their own program. SPD/Green coalitions sat in Lower Saxony and West Berlin, and moderizing SPD leaders like Lafontaine held the premiership in former CDU strongholds such as Schleswig-Holstein, Lower Saxony, and the Saarland. In a 1989 report to an SPD program commission, Lafontaine issued four objectives: ecological conversion of industry, strengthening social democratic politics internationally, gender equality, and a restructuring of work. All of these objectives were adopted in the SPD's official Berlin Program in December of that year.[2] Unions opposed Lafontaine's proposal for a shortened workweek because it included corresponding pay cuts. Lafontaine may have elicited new middle-class support, though, since he had a environmentally based solution for unemployment.

The *Grünen*'s program concentrated more strictly than before on issues of environmental protection.[3] It also supported women's rights to economic equality, a shortened workweek (though without pay cuts), and democratization of production. Hence the *Grüne* alternative program no longer really represented a clear alternative, and their work-centered reading of ecology had been absorbed by the other party. The SPD score did fall some thirty points behind that of the bourgeois coalition (i.e., the CDU/CSU combined received 54.8 percent, vs. 24.3 percent for the SPD). Yet 600,000 of the Greens' voters defected to the SPD—15 percent of the latter's 1987 Bundestag election vote.

The Cataclysm: France

The French Legislative elections of March 1993 saw a reckoning between the public and the party that had occupied the government for ten of the last twelve years. The return of the Right to power and a Socialist debacle seemed to approach with the inevitability of a force of nature. Presiding over record levels of unemployment, the PS lost whatever credibility it still had as agent for social change. With mounting scandals, even their default claim that they were the most competent managers of all the leading parties was bankrupt. In that context, it was rational that the ecologists should continue to keep their distance from the Socialists.

In formal terms, the combined forces of French ecology now stood squarely behind the autonomy strategy first advanced by the *Verts*. With a combined score of almost 15 percent in the 1992 Regionals, the ecologists realized they had more to gain by putting up a united front in the next elections than by airing their many differences in strategy. *Génération Ecologie* and *Les Verts* signed an alliance contract, the *Entente Écologiste*, in November 1992. The two parties agreed to run only one ecological candidate in each district in the Legislative elections.That meant that alliances between ecology and any leading or alternative party were ruled out in advance. Despite this formal autonomy, however, the *Verts* suddenly moved away from their strict emphasis on environmental themes. They decided during the campaign of the fall of 1992 to downplay demands for environmental protection in favor of issues traditionally associated with the Left, work and unemployment. They wanted to address charges that French political ecology had no comprehensive vision of society, that it was about more than just cleaning up the environment, and that they had a solution to disturbingly high levels of unemployement. As Prendiville notes, however, the *Verts* may have lacked credibility when they addressed themes outside of environmental protection alone.[4] The actions of the PS itself contributed to this credibility problem. Two months before the election, Michel Rocard, the PS's presumed presidential candidate for 1995, made a daring new initiative known as the "Big Bang" for its suddenness and political impact. Seeing his own party gravely threatened, Rocard called for a total political and ideological recomposition of the Left that would integrate ecologists with progressive elements of the PCF and PS. In addition, Rocard uncannily echoed the *Verts*' discourse of the previous fall with a proposal for work sharing. Rocard's endorsement of the ecologists' ideas, coupled with the hope he instilled that the PS might simply dissolve and regroup with the ecologists, assured the latter's association with the Socialists. Since the outcome of the election was judged as a defeat for the PS rather than a victory for the Right, the association was unfortunate (and did not help the Socialists at any rate: they hit a historic low of 18 percent).

Furthermore, all the prospects of sharing power, fed by favorable early polls, created an irresistable temptation for the leaders of the two ecology parties. There were negotiations with representatives of the centrist and center-right parties, during which both Lalonde and Waechter seriously entertained proposals for the ecologists to join an incoming center-right government. Adding to the confusion, Lalonde said at one point that he would accept the Socialists' offer to join in the recomposition led by Rocard. Yet he recanted within a week. This association with all the leading parties of government was widely judged after the elections—by many ecologists as well as political commentators—to have compromised the ecologists' antisystem identity.

Lalonde's handling of the 1993 Legislative campaign contradicted the claims upon which he built his party's reputation. Promising effective leadership, he vacillated. Though he proffered an electoralist green party, he was widely regarded as having blown the election for the greens. Lalonde thus faced a rebellion from within his party's own ranks, and GE never approached its scores in the 1992 Regionals. As for the *Verts*, the autonomy strategy had run its course. The Socialists, facing a huge right-wing majority in the National Assembly, would soon shift their own strategy by claiming the mantle of opposition to the status quo. Recognizing that shift, the *Verts* militants gave the majority to the left-ecologists, now headed by Dominique Voynet, who advocated a dialogue with progressive portions of the French Left.

The twin cataclysms spurred change in the socialist parties and, after some confusion, their rejuvenation. Lafontaine's successor Bjorn Engholm was forced to step down in the midst of a scandal. The next chancellor candidate, Rudolf Scharping, a conservative, fell short of unseating the CDU/CSU/FDP coalition. The more progressive Lafontaine regained control of the party by assuming the chairmanship in November 1995. Rocard took over the PS after the March 1993 French Legislatives. Long associated with the PS's neoliberal turn, he failed to provide sorely needed inspiration for the party's militant base. Rocard's successor, Henri Emanuelli, then resigned in scandal in 1995. After that the party was headed by Lionel Jospin, who ran a surprisingly strong, though unsuccessful presidential campaign that year. The changes in the two socialist parties have restored their fortunes, and thus they still pose a challenge to the greens' identities.

After the Deluge: Strategic Transformation in Germany

Crisis also cleared the way for changes in the leadership composition of the two green parties. Each one is now moving at least partly in the direction the other embraced before the two cataclysmic elections. The *Grünen* have been quite successful. They began to define their identity more strictly around environmental protection during this period. Nevertheless, they have not sacrificed efficacy, since they now participate in regional alliances, and did so by rallying a large base of electoral support. They have renounced the party's earlier anticapitalist position and turned toward proposals to reform liberal economics in a greener direction. The program for the 1994 Federal Elections, adopted at Mannheim during that year, proposed environmental taxes, energy conversion, and ecologically based job creation programs. The last item, which has been on the *Grünen*'s agenda for many years, has been put in practice. Recycling programs first introduced by the *Grüne*-sponsored legislation in several *Länder*, and now implemented in Hesse and North Rhine-Westphalia, have created tens of thousands of jobs, in an industry that generates 100 million Deutschmarks per year, and has a 10 percent yearly growth rate. That achievement helps the *Grünen* counter the perennial charge that environmental protection and job growth are mutually exclusive.

Along with this change in programmatic emphasis, there has been a change in the way the *Grüne* program is disseminated to the public. In 1991, an alliance between the *Aufbruch* group and the realists gained a clear majority in the *Grünen*, whereas the last of the fundamentalists departed with Jutta Ditfurth in 1991. The *Aufbruch* strategy had been to alleviate the party's debilitating factional squabbles and create a more structured, professional internal organization. Since that current's ascendancy, the Greens have fine-tuned their approach to the media. They retained an advertising agency to redesign their campaign materials and to coordinate events and programs for maximum public relations impact. This strategy has targeted the Greens' most reliable core supporters, first-time and youthful voters, with issues they clearly favor, such as environmental protection.[5]

In light of their current emphasis on material questions, and on work and employment in particular, it could be argued that the *Grünen* are still as red as they are green. In addition, they take positions on many issues that fall in some sense to the Left of the SPD and bourgeois parties. They favor withdrawal from NATO, for example, strong regulation of business, an exit from nuclear power, and the rights of culturally marginal groups such as immigrants or gays. The crucial break with the past, however, is that they have rejected the Marxist scaffolding on which these themes once rested. Along with that, they had abandoned their assumption that they could simply ride the wave of an immanent crisis of capitalism spurred by a mass-based popular movement toward a greener society. One indication of their shift toward a tacit acceptance of market economics is the *Grünen*'s endorsement of European integration according to the terms of the Maastricht Treaty, on the grounds that it sets up a political structure for environmental policy and (perhaps paradoxically), because it may protect Europe from the harshest winds of global trade and currency speculation.[6] Another indication of their turn away from socialism was the party's official refusal to cooperate in the Bundestag with the Party of Democratic Socialism (PDS), the remnant of the East German Communist Party, at the Mannheim Conference (the Greens and SPD have sometimes worked with the PDS in practice, though).

The *Grünen*'s organizational and programmatic changes have cleared the obstacles to alliances with other parties. As in the 1980s, the sheer size and heterogeneity of the *Grünen*'s electoral base have created many opportunities for alliances. The Mannheim Conference sanctioned participation in a government coalition, including the federal government. That goal has become reality in several *Länder:* Hesse, North Rhine-Westphalia, Schleswig-Holstein, and in Saxony-Anhalt in the former East Germany. Even Black/Green (Christian Democrat/Green) coalitions are not out of the question: the idea has been advanced by both Kohl and Fischer. With Kohl and the conservatives' popularity strained by their ruthless march toward European Monetary Union, the prospect that a Red/Green coalition may form the Federal Government after the 1998 elections is likely.

The *Grünen* have begun an impressive rebound since the adoption of their pure green strategy and new professional profile. In the elections to the Federal Parliament in 1994, the *Grünen*, now allied with the Greens of the eastern *Länder*, won 7.3 percent of the vote and 49 seats. The most striking *Grüne* victories occurred in *Landtag* elections in the spring of 1995. In Bremen, they pulled in 13.1 percent, up from 11.4 percent in 1991. In North Rhine-Westphalia, Germany's most populous state, the Greens won 10 percent, up from 5 percent in 1990. The FDP fared far worse in the course of these events: its vote shrank to 3.4 percent (vs. 9.5 percent in 1991) in Bremen, and to 4 percent (vs. 5.8 percent) in North Rhine-Westphalia, prompting the resignation of party chairman and current Foreign Minister Klaus Kinkel. The results of the *Landtag* elections have prompted the expectation that the *Grünen* will replace the FDP in its traditional role as the pivotal force in the German party system and the kingmaker that determines the ruling alliance.

If the Greens had the advantage of a clear identity in this period of resurgence, however, it may still be due as much to the SPD strategy as to their own. The Social Democrats, as they did a decade before, turned to the Right. Rudolf Scharping, chancellor candidate in 1994, campaigned on a pro-business, pro-Atlantic platform with the aim of reassuring centrist voters. As part of this strategy, Scharping refused to endorse the idea of an SPD/Green alliance in Bonn, and he distanced himself from the greens' policies. With mounting public disenchantment with Kohl and the costs of German unification, Scharping's approach may indeed have worked, but for his own blunders and lack of charisma. The SPD had 38 percent, with just ten seats short of a relative majority needed to form a government. Once more, the SPD ceded postindustrial territory to the Greens. The reconstructed, pragmatic *Grünen* of the 1990s may therefore have one thing in common with the radical *Grünen* of the 1980s. Then as now, their position and success were owed not so much to a planned strategy as simply occupying a void left open by the socialist party. That space might be contested again by the new leadership of the SPD. After taking over from Scharping, the politically flexible Lafontaine has moved his party to the Left. Lafontaine has generally moved to challenge Kohl's moves to dismantle the German welfare state in time for the projected currency union in 1999. Like Lafontaine, Gerhard Schröder has strong credentials in the area of the environment, with the advantage that he is viewed as a more attractive chancellor candidate in the elections of 1998. As polls now show, he would become Germany's next chancellor, should he be selected by his party. In a government with Schröder at its head, the Greens could appear as an appendage to it, rather than a force for change and opposition.

After the Deluge: Strategic
Transformation in France

With the cataclysm of the 1993 Legislative elections behind them, the *Verts* moved in a red/green direction. A new majority steering the party after December 1993 stated its "openness to discussion" with political forces then comprising the opposition in France: the Socialists, Communists, and other small parties of the Left or Center-Left. The change in strategy showed prescience, and perhaps a bit of luck.The ensuing dialogue culminated in the signing in March 1997 of an electoral and programmatic accord between the *Verts* and the Socialists. The intervening period had seen a tightening of political links between the parties of the Left and a renewed commitment to left-wing discourse across the board. This Left was suddenly swept back into power after President Chirac called early parliamentary elections in June of that year.

For several years after the left-ecological majority began to lead the party, the *Verts* had asserted that they, and not the Socialists, were now the true bearers of the values of the Left. Dominque Voynet, leader of the new majority, was never one to forget the disappointments and reversals during the years when the Socialists had held power, nor sparing in her criticism of Jospin when he began to lead the party. Voynet clearly leaned toward the Left in her own positions. She had opposed the Maastricht Treaty (which the PS had helped negotiate) during the referendum on the issue in the fall of 1992. The program for her 1995 presidential campaign proposed to start a massive public works program to stimulate jobs, expand the criteria for the *Revenu Minimum d'Insertion* (a guaranteed minimum wage for job-seekers instituted by the Rocard government), and to create a minimum wage for students. In addition, the program reiterated the *Verts'* calls for work sharing with no corresponding pay cuts. This shift toward a left-ecological program, however, showed no immediate sign that it could reverse the *Verts'* declining scores. In 1994, they received 2.6 percent in the Cantonal elections, and 2.9 percent in the European Parliament elections. Voynet, a candidate for the presidency in 1995, received only 3.32 percent on the first round of voting.

The change in the *Verts'* fortunes owed as much to changes in the Socialist Party as to that of the ecologists themselves. After scoring surprisingly well in the 1995 Presidential elections, Jospin became Party Secretary and began a much-needed renewal. He moved to democratize the party, to check the influence of factions on party programs, to involve activists more fully in party affairs, and to place more women in key positions. Jospin also shifted the programmatic direction of the PS, asserting his "right to take inventory" of the neoliberal turn in the later Mitterrand years, and adopting an increasingly critical stance toward the Gaullist governments' handling of the fiscal targets for European Monetary Union. Jospin also aimed to restore the sympathy and support of other parties of the Left. These included the Communists, themselves undergoing a prodemocratic thaw, the *Mouvement des Citoyens*, led by former PS member Jean-Pierre Chevènement, the *Parti Radical-Socialiste* (the former *Mouvement Radicale du Gauche*, a center-left sattelite to the PS), ecological splinter parties such as AREV and CES, and the *Verts*—all of whom responded with tentative support for Jospin, and who were also engaged in countless bilateral negotiations on coalition strategy by this point.

The *Verts*, perhaps because they had few other useful options, finally accepted the Socialists' overtures with the signing of the electoral pact in 1997. The *Verts* would receive thirty-one districts where the Socialists would present no candidate in the first round of the voting on May 24th, in exchange for seventy-five of the same for the Socialists (some of those ceded by the Socialists went to ecologists from the splinter green parties). The accords centered on the institution of a thirty-five-hour work week, along with the cessation of infrastructure and energy projects such as the Rhine-Rhône canal and the nuclear plant at Malville. Jospin had proposed the fusion of the Ministries of the Environment and of Regional Policy during his 1995 Presidential run, and that too became an item of the 1997 accord with the *Verts*.

At around the same time, Voynet and Chevènement had helped convince Socialists and Communists to resolve their differences on European integration, and the outcome pulled the PS itself to the Left. The Socialists signed a programmatic accord with the Communists a month after the *Verts*/PS agreement. The Communists would relax their firm opposition to the Maastricht timetable. In exchange, the PS agreed to several qualifying conditions on France's entry into EMU, such as the creation of a political entity to parallel the European Central Bank, and the admission of countries with weaker currencies, such as Italy. The PS campaign, further, emphasized growth and employment over fiscal austerity, and state leadership over laissez-faire policies in the labor market. French voters, haunted by unemployment, rejected the prospect of further pain for the sake of placating German fears of a soggy eurocurrency. Above all, they sanctioned the Juppé government for its failure to explain to them how they would benefit from monetary integration. With 330 seats in an assembly of 577 seats, they gave the Left (i.e., the PS and allies, the Communists, and the ecologists) a strong mandate for change. The Right suffered its worst scores in thirty years (the RPR and UDF together lost 229 seats, leaving only 235). While the president normally holds the supreme executive power in the French system, Chirac gravely weakened his own mandate.[7] The new Prime Minister and his junior partners would thus have extraordinary political stature. While Chirac's role is now limited to foreign affairs, Jospin is running the country.

The *Verts*, then, became a part of a powerful and strikingly left-wing governing majority. Voynet gave up her new seat representing the town of Dole, in the Jura, to become the new Minister of the Environment and Regional Policy. The ecologists thus had seven seats rather than eight in parliament, though the new ministry would seem to be more than enough compensation.[8] The developments were a personal victory for Voynet and her left-ecological perspective. The *Verts'* representation in the National Assembly is the reward for more than twenty years of perserverance for some of the new deputies. We should note, however, the *Verts'* red/green strategy has not necessarily received a resounding affirmation by their electorate or party rank-and-file. At 6.81

percent, the ecologists' electoral scores are close to those in the last elections, in which the autonomy strategy still prevailed. Further, the *Vert*/Socialist pact was approved by a majority of only twelve hundred in a party assembly of only twenty-one hundred members (notably, the party's Paris regional branch did not approve it). Many in the party were skeptical about renewing it for the next elections of the Regional Councils in March 1998. As it turned out, there was a united *Verts*/Socialist/Communist list (dubbed *Gauche Plurielle*, or "Diverse Left") in only 55 of the 92 departments in which the *Verts* ran any candidates at all. Further, the *Verts'* own results were decent but unencouraging: they won 68 council seats and 5.6 percent of the vote, down from 106 seats and 6.8 percent in the 1992 Regional elections.

Finally, Voynet will have to act out the full drama of holding a major position in government while leading a party with an oppositional culture, before the *Verts'* electorate can speak again on the issue. There are many hurdles: the contradiction between active regional development and environmental protection, and, more critically, the junior status of her post *vis-à-vis* the Ministry of Transport. That post went to Communist Jean-Claude Gayssot, a member of a party that has now reformed in many ways, but is still likely to view bulldozers and concrete as instruments of human progress. Still more poignant is the fact that Dominique Strauss-Kahn, the powerful new Minister of Finance, Trade, and Economics, has close personal ties with many of the top figures in the nuclear power industry.

In both Germany and France, ecological strategies changed as the status of the Socialist Party changed. As the SPD began to make forays into postindustrial thematic territory, the *Grünen*, like the *Verts* in a similar situation earlier, stressed their core issue, the environment. When the PS, in a similar position to the SPD in the period between 1983 and 1987 failed to redefine their mission, it was rational for the greens to try to occupy a space for a left-leaning oppositional force. It remains to be seen how the *Grünen* will fare if the SPD turns in the future toward postindustrial themes, as they did during the cataclysmic election of 1990, or if the *Verts* will damage their identity by participating in a left-wing government, as the Waechterians once feared. We shall discuss these prospects further in the Conclusion. Let us turn to suggest the relevance of the strategic interaction framework for other national cases.

Applying the Framework: Socialist/Green Relations in Europe

In the United Kingdom, Austria, and Belgium major patterns in socialist/green relations resemble those in France and West Germany, respectively. Italy represents a negative case, where, in light of conditions that resemble those in France, the greens adopted a flawed strategy. Sweden and the Netherlands provide material for partial comparison, where one or the other of our two components of an effective strategy was absent. In all of these cases, the background conditions that held for the French and West German cases still obtain—that is, the growth of a relatively young, new middle-class electorate, an activist cohort interested in postindustrial issues, and the corresponding potential for volatility or decline in the leading socialist party's overall support.[9]

Long-range trends in Britain from about 1979 to 1992 are comparable to those we have observed in France in about the same time period. Like the PS, the British Labour Party combined attributes of identity and efficacy. With a strong class identity, coupled with a fairly radical platform, Labour had been the main national political vehicle for opposition to the status quo in Britain, and groups with a variety of political identities and agendas have operated within it. It embraced postindustrial themes and thus limited the possibilities for a progressive challenge built upon it. Labour held the support of the Campaign for Nuclear Disarmament and attracted antinuclear sentiment with proposals for unilateral disarmament and exit from NATO for its 1983 General Election campaign.[10] New Left activists with a democratic socialist agenda, such as the Trotskyist Militant group, also influenced the leadership, pulling it to the Left. Radicals that might otherwise have flowed into an alternative opposition party (as was the case with the *Grünen*) stayed within the fold of the major socialist party (as was the case in France until about 1978).

Labour has traditionally been the trade union movement's major voice in the political sphere. The Trades Union Congress

(TUC) exerted an unusually strong influence on the parliamentary party, through funding, leadership selection, and voting on platforms. For our purposes, it does not matter that Labour was in opposition for this entire period. After 1979, Labour's opposition status allowed militants to move the party to the Left. Official Labour platforms included proposals for nationalization of industry until the 1990s. After 1986, Labour leaders Neil Kinnock and Tony Blair moved to check the trade unions' influence over the party's parliamentary leadership and to project a far more moderate identity. Yet the majoritarian bias in the party system still makes life difficult for the Greens, who may also attract moderate supporters with environmental concern. Even more than the PS, which had to face the Communist Party, Labour has commanded the Left and the Center during the period in which the Greens have competed in elections.

Since Labour combined identity and efficacy, green politics has been weak in Great Britain, weaker still than in France. With one notable exception, nationwide scores for the British Green Party (formed in 1973 and then known as the People's Party) averaged around 2 percent during the period in question.[11] Activists in the Green Party clearly recognized their unfavorable situation. They responded with the type of strategy we might expect: an emphasis on identity. As early as 1974, they deliberately expunged socialist themes in their platform and concentrated on pure ecological principles.[12] Since that time, they have developed these principles into a radical ecological program, which includes a strong commitment to direct democracy and pluralism, resembling that of the *Verts*. Their membership tends to come from the environmental movement. Left-wing activists have remained more pro-Labour, and progrowth in their orientation.[13]

The outcome of the 1989 elections to the European Parliament suggests that this pure green strategy fits the situation in the British party system. The greens scored almost 15 percent nationwide, and over 20 percent in seventeen divisions in England. This occurred despite the fact that a recently reformed Labour Party was quite competitive, and tactical votes might have flowed to it. But Labour campaigned largely on the issue of economic policy and the Thatcher administration's record in it. In addition, Labour had abandoned its one greenish issue, unilateral nuclear disarmament. In this situation, it was clearly strategic for the Greens to identify themselves with pure environmental themes, their main point of comparative advantage. The 1992 General Election saw a resurgence of the Liberal party, which had a program of parliamentary reform and civil rights, and is thus the closest to the radically democratic Greens in its outlook. The latter's score thus fell to 1 percent. Due to British ecology's perennially bad scores, many environmental activists have preferred to concentrate on social movement activity—an identity strategy carried to its most extreme conclusion.

Just as the situation in the United Kingdom resembles that in France, socialist/green relations in Austria from 1971 to 1992 reflect those in West Germany from 1974 to 1987. At a point when postindustrial demands first entered political discourse, the *Sozialdemokratische Partei Österreichs* (SPÖ) tended toward efficacy, sacrificing identity. Led by Dr. Bruno Kreisky, the SPÖ held an absolute majority in the Austrian legislature, the *Nationalrat* from 1971 until 1983. Maximizing votes and organizational power, it rejected new social movement issues and progressive reform programs. The SPÖ party organization has an unusually high penetration into many branches of the state and economy. That meant strong membership and administrative links with the Austrian Federation of Labor Unions. The latter took a conservative, progrowth outlook and opposed the mobilization of New Left activists within the party. As in the Federal Republic of Germany, there was no Communist Party to serve as an alternative pole for left-wing opposition to the leading Socialist Party.

As we argued with respect to the West German case, the tensions in a strategy of efficacy on the part of the Socialist Party are intensified by government tenure, and that ultimately creates a favorable situation for progressive challengers. It allows the new party to maximize efficacy without sacrificing identity. Like the *Grünen*, the Austrian Greens (the *Vereinte Grüne Österreichs*, or VGÖ; and the *Alternative Liste Österreichs*, or ALÖ) began to draw votes away in 1983, after the Socialist Party had stumbled over popular opposition to its nuclear power program. Like the *Grünen*, the Austrian Greens, especially the more radical ALÖ, fused elements of a left-wing program with those of the environmental movement. Their 1987 platform included a strong antisystem, anticapitalist defining identity, with a program of nationalization and guaranteed basic income.[14] Like the *Grünen*, the Austrian Greens drew younger, new middle-class voters away from the SPÖ, and also radical activists from the party organization, contributing to the SPÖ's defeat in 1986. The ecology parties performed relatively well, with 4.8 percent and eight seats in 1986; 4.8 percent and ten seats in 1990; and with 4.81 percent and nine seats in 1995. They have since united to become *Die Grünen—Die Grüne Alternative.*

The situation in Belgium in many respects resembles that in Germany and Austria. The socialist parties, the Flemish *Socialistische Partij* (SP) and the Walloon *Parti Socialiste* (PS), have a working-class base and fairly traditional social democratic programs (especially the latter). Further, they have generally failed to address postindustrial themes.[15] The green parties, *Ecolo* (Walloon) and *Agalev* (Flemish) have a left-ecological program, though they are more moderate than the *Grünen* during the 1980s. The Belgian ecologists have placed emphasis on social themes. Their programs are sharply critical of international political economic organizations such as GATT or the plans for EMU stipulated in the Maastricht treaty. They have worked to oppose plant closings, privatizations, and youth unemployment. In addition, they have sought contacts with trade unions, and have formed a tentative legislative alliance with the PS in the Walloon Regional Chamber.[16] This social element of their program, however, is coupled with positions on a wide range of environmental policy issues, and with the characteristically green isssue of prodemocratic institutional reform. With this moderate left-ecological strategy, they have achieved some of the highest scores for any green party in Europe.Their combined vote in the 1989 European elections, for example, was 16 percent, and *Ecolo* scored 13.5 percent alone in the national parliamentary elections of 1991. Their combined vote dropped slightly in the 1994 European Parliament and 1995 Belgian National Parliament elections, to 11.5 percent and 10 percent, respectively.[17]

The moderation of the Belgian ecologists relative to the Marxist-influenced program of the *Grünen* in a similar period may be explained in part with a closer look at the profile of the socialist parties. The Belgian Socialists have not fully undergone the challenges from either the neoliberal assault on the welfare state or the mobilization of the New Left that the SPD faced in the early 1980s. The elaborate system of interregional compromise under the Belgian federalist system has maintained a high level of welfare state expenditure, particularly to support depressed industries in the Francophone region. In the 1995 National elections, the SP and PS had strong scores—despite the taint of years of corruption scandals—since they portrayed themselves as the defenders of Belgium's social security system. Further, during the mid-1980s, the Socialists, then in opposition, did embrace some postindustrial issues, such as peace, populist grassroots movements, and ecology. Thus they have defended a core working-class identity, yet addressed efficacy as well, by defending the entitlements of a range of middle-class citizens, and by showing some openness to postindustrial themes. In this situation, we might expect that *Ecolo* and *Agalev* would not advance a strongly left-wing reading of ecology, since the socialists themselves still defended the core features of the welfare state. If there is some overlap between the ecologists' left-ecological identity and the left-wing position of the Socialists, that could explain the slight decline in the ecologists' scores, precisely at a point in 1995 when the Socialists underwent a resurgence on the basis of those themes.

Socialist parties in Sweden and the Netherlands, like those in West Germany and Austria, have institutionalized ties with strong, fairly unified trade union movements. Yet the Swedish and Dutch socialists moved in the direction of identity during the period in question. As we would expect, that narrowed the set of strategic options for the ecology parties. In Sweden, the Social Democratic Party (SAP), possessed many attributes of efficacy. It had a strong union/party linkage, a vast membership, and a nearly hegemonic position as the party of government for all but four years of the period after 1968. Yet, at a critical point, it leaned toward identity, by advancing a radical reform program on behalf of a particular movement constituency. Trade union leaders put party leaders under pressure to adopt the Meidner Plan, in which wage earners could gradually acquire shares in their firms—a measure whose logical conclusion was the socialization of industry. If the SAP leaned toward a radical identity, however, it was with a specific movement in mind; and that movement resisted many issues of interest to the New Left such as opposition to nuclear power. In other words, there was a window of opportunity for a challenger to advance radically green or postindustrial issues.

Accordingly, the Swedish environmental party, *Miljöpartiet*, chose a pure ecological strategy. Like the *Verts*, it defined its identity by rejecting any placement in the Left/Right dimension. Like the *Verts*, it had a comprehensive program for decentralization and global solidarity and peace. It refused to support the socialist-inspired Meidner Plan.Yet *Miljöpartiet* did not fully reap the reward from this maneuver, since it failed to fully distinguish itself *vis-à-vis* potential competitors on the Left. It had an alternative program, but lacked a defining identity. Despite its pure ecological identity, *Miljöpartiet* consistently joined legislative coalitions with the Swedish Communists (by then renamed the Left Party). The latter incorporated New Left issues such as participatory themes and opposition to nuclear power during the 1970s. Another problem for *Miljöpartiet* was that it tacitly identified itself with the SAP itself when it refused to support a Conservative-led government in 1991. Therefore, *Miljöpartiet* has done well only when extraordinary factors made an ecological theme, opposition to nuclear power, one of the most salient ones in a national election (with 5.5 percent in 1988, it cleared the threshold for representation in the Swedish parliament). Given the situation in Sweden, *Miljöpartiet* should avoid any suggestion of coalition with the hegemonic SAP, and at the same time perhaps merge with the Left Party (provided the latter in turn reforms in a still greener direction).

In the Netherlands, the *Partij van der Arbeit* (PvdA) sacrificed efficacy for identity. Yet the movement it identified itself with was not the same as that which the SAP addressed. The PvdA moved not toward the Left but the New Left. In the early 1970s, weakening of patronage ties between Dutch parties and public institutions resulted, for the PdvA, in weakened union ties. At the same time, New Left activists began to enter the party and shift its agenda in a progressive direction. During the 1980s, the PdvA thus gained a positive image regarding the issues of concern to new middle-class voters, including the peace movement and the environment.[18] Knowing this much, we might expect that an ecology party in the Netherlands would have difficulties. Indeed, *Groen Links* (Green Left, which united Social Christians, Pacifists, Independent Socialists, and Communists; earlier known as the Green Progressive Accord) has never scored more than 5 percent of the vote even in a system of proportional representation.

Nevertheless, there is evidence this red/green fusion was still more viable in the context of Dutch party competition than a pure green strategy. Despite its modest scores, *Groen Links* did far better than a party with a pure green identity, *De Groenen*, which hardly ever surpassed 1 percent.[19] In addition, more favorable scores for *Groen Links* appeared as the PvdA shed the socialist elements of its platform and courted centrist voters in 1986. That left room for the red/green party to advance slightly in National Parliament elections in 1989, with 4.1 percent of the vote, up from 3.3 percent in 1986, and 7 percent in the European elections that year. Despite this opportunity, *Groen Links* may have faltered because it did not translate this left-ecological identity into an alternative program. Internal factions, the remnants of the heterogeneous party organizations that merged to form *Groen Links*, were unable to agree on issues such as a social policy, environmental taxes, and a guaranteed basic income.[20]

The situation in Italy resembles that of France and Great Britain. The Left combined attributes of efficacy and identity, constraining the options for the Greens. In Italy, of course, the "Left" refers not to one party, but an array of New Left, Center-Left, and Communist parties. For the Italian Greens, however, the strategic situation was virtually the same as that of the *Verts*, who faced a party system pulled to the Left by a large Communist Party. The *Partito Comunista Italiano* (PCI) was permanently excluded from government, though it was strongly implanted at the local level. It straddled red and green, advocating working-class goals while opposing nuclear power. Further, in Italy, pure proportional representation encourages new entrants to the Italian party system. Thus a variety of progressive and left-leaning party system positions were already occupied. Smaller parties like the Radicals and Proletarian Democracy took proenvironmental and radically democratic positions. After corruption scandals shook the leading parties of the center (the Italian Socialist Party and the Christian Democrats), the left-wing parties positioned themselves on the side of political and institutional reform, coopting another typical issue for the greens.[21] Given this situation, we might expect that the Italian ecologists, like the *Verts*, might have to struggle to assert their own identity. What the Federation of Green Lists actually did was advance a red/green fusion instead. New Left activists and center environmentalists had united to form the *Liste Verdi* in

1986. Though there were conflicts over the issue, their platform included social demands with environmental issues. A former member summed up their identity problem: the greens were simply the "umpteenth tiny party of the Left."[22] Hence, even under proportional representation, and despite ruptures in leading parties like the PCI, they have rarely scored over 3 percent in a national elections, nor over 4 percent in a regional one.

The evidence from these additional cases suggests that the status of the socialist parties is a major determinant of the greens' strategy and trajectory, as we have argued throughout. The latter's successes correlate with their adoption of a clear strategic alternative to the socialists. Further work could apply this framework to each national case in more depth. That would permit a closer examination of the iterated games between greens and socialists over time, and a comparison of the electoral scores of each party in successive elections to guage the results. Furthermore, additional cases would allow intervening factors to be considered which we have held constant or subsumed into our main variables. These might include electoral, parliamentary or administrative institutions; the composition of the government at each juncture; the greens' relations with either communist, centrist, or right-wing parties; and the impact of the fall of the Cold War, the rise of the parties of the far Right, and the process of European integration on party systems overall.

The survey suggests another trend. Many Western European green parties now lean toward a pure ecological strategy (without necessarily following the strict fundamentalist line of the *Verts* between 1988 and 1993). The Belgian Greens have framed moderate left-wing demands within a basically environmentalist worldview. The Italian Green Lists might clearly have benefited by adhering closely to a pure green identity. Even the *Grünen*, long the most influential of European green parties, have moved in a pure green direction, and appear to have benefitted from it. Only the *Verts*—paradoxically, due to their earlier identification with the pure green strategy—have moved in the opposite direction. In the Conclusion, we discuss the prospects for these transformed strategies, in a changed political landscape now shaped by European integration and the simultaneous political resurgence of the SPD and PS. We also present a final critique of the fundamental strategic choices of identity and efficacy.

Chapter Ten

Conclusion

The conflict over whether protest organizations should participate in formal parliamentary institutions has divided progessive politics since the inception of democratic institutions themselves. It was present at the dawn of the workers' movement and the simultaneous struggle for representative rights, for example, within the Chartist movement in Britain and among the forces leading the February Revolution of 1848 in France. The debate exacerbated the schism between the Second and Third Internationals in the early part of this century. It persisted in the antagonism between Communist and Social Democratic parties during the Cold War. Today, even the most pragmatic exponents of the environmental movement have sometimes had to wonder whether the ecologists' newly won responsibilities as participants in government threaten their own identity as popular tribunes or environmental gadflies. Taking stock of these debates, and the theories that have developed along with them, we have advanced our own model of the strategic choices involved.

Parties with ties to radical social movements face a choice between two imperatives. With identity, the party gestures toward an independent social movement for its legitimacy. Thus it elevates a special part of society to the status of a universal model for social change. With efficacy, the party signifies its responsibility to the polity rather than to one part of it. It seeks coalition and fusion rather than doctrinal purity and independence, programmatic breadth rather than depth and coherence, and strength in numbers rather than true commitment. While all progresssive parties may try to maximize both imperatives, the *Verts* stressed identity and movement, and the *Grünen* often tended toward fusion and coalition.

We have also asked what the options are when not one but two types of transformative organizations compete for the authority to guide progressive politics. While the ecologists claim greater legitimacy, socialist parties have superior power. Hence the more established parties' strategic course structures the opportunities and choices for the ecological challengers. When socialist parties can maximize both identity and efficacy, the ecologists' options narrow. They are not necessarily foreclosed, but the greens may need to stress identity that much more. That must be an identity that the opposing force has never fully addressed (such as the environmental movement itself, in the French context). Where socialist parties have tended to sacrifice identity for efficacy, the choices may be more open for the ecology party. It may be easier for the greens to claim outsider status in situations where socialists have long been inside the political system. Occupation of government, or close competition for it, aggravate movement/party tensions in the socialist coalition. When the latter starts to disintegrate, there are simply more available partners for the greens, and it may be thus convenient for the greens to fuse the more radical socialist thematic material with postindustrial demands.

Looking Toward the Future:
Competition in the Progressive Arena

Socialist parties still pose a challenge to the greens' ability to define themselves within European party systems. It is true that the former have their own identity problems. In the past decade or so, they have had to move further and further away from the representation of strictly class-based socioeconomic demands and state instruments meant to further them. On the other hand, their more recent embrace of neoliberalism has clearly risked their credibility by identifying them with the policies of the bourgeois parties. With the socialists thus squeezed, however, the greens' own problems may begin. Socialists may try to identify themselves with greens' typical concerns: environmental issues themselves, political and civil rights, and the defense of welfare entitlements (the last now reaching a crescendo with the political backlash against EMU).

Socialist leaders in France and Germany, recognizing public support for proenvironmental policies, have either brought members of the ecology parties into government, or propose to do so. The political subtext behind the socialist rhetoric surrounding their friendly embrace of the environmentalist movement is that the greens are there as specialists in environmental issues—and are thus subliminally portrayed as partisans of a narrow "single-issue" movement. After all, socialist politicians can hardly be expected to take a contrasting position, to the effect that the greens represent a broad popular opposition capable of replacing the Socialist Party itself. In addition, green ministers often find themselves in junior positions, wherein they discover that a lack of means is coupled with the inevitable compromise of the virtuous ends. While few of the leaders of the ecology parties would deny that forcing the leading parties to address their themes is a significant accomplishment, they have to face the perennial problem of issue-theft by the established parties. Cooptation of green themes may undermine the public perception of a need for a separate organization to advance them, and, with that, momentum toward environmental reform that is greater than that which the established parties can be expected to support.

The problems may be compounded by the fact that the greens themselves have recently moved toward an electoralist model. The green parties in France and Germany have become politically decoupled from the environmental movements that once supported them, and they are not parties of mass membership. In this respect, they have tended to move toward efficacy: they have broad support, mobilized mainly at each election. Without intensely committed support of popular movements, then, there is always the question as to whether that support is broad but not deep or reliable. Since electoral campaigns are the main interface between party and public, furthermore, it is always possible that their identity may be defined by their electoral competitors.

The *Grünen*, now the third force in German politics, have negotiated these tricky circumstances with great skill. They have redefined their identity around environmental themes while also delivering tangible results. With a more professional, coherent party structure, the *Grünen* were in a better position to transmit their identity to groups likely to identify with their themes, such as young service sector workers, who can now easily see their concerns reflected in the party's agenda.[1] As participants in *Land* governments, the Greens have sponsored ecological investment programs, redeeming their earlier promises to bring about a greener, more humane political economy. They have projected identity, yet with maximum efficacy.

Still, aspects of the *Grünen's* efficacy may conflict with their identity in the future. Their openness to alliance with the moderate Right, along with the moderate Left, leaves questions as to their commitment to basic principles. The responsibility of holding power itself, as always, poses risks for their identity as a voice of criticism of the regime in Bonn. Fischer himself recognizes this difficulty: even in the midst of their current wave of successes and alliances, "voters expect us to keep pushing them [i.e., environmental demands] higher up on the agenda and act as a forceful opposition."[2] Fischer, avatar of green realism, is implying that his party's own interests lie in cooperation—and at the same time in antagonism. Still more crucial is the fact that the *Grünen* owe their identity as an oppositional force partly to the conservative stance and vacillating leadership of the Social Democrats. Should the latter's position change, the *Grünen's* support may decline in response. That is not unlikely, furthermore, if the chancellorship is won by the SPD's Gerhard Schröder, a charismatic figure with strong credentials on the environment and other postindustrial issues. Two forces would thus compete to project an identity as representatives of the environment and postindustrial issues, despite the fact that they seek the combined strength to form the next government in Bonn. On top of that, the Right will argue, pejoratively, that they maximize "identity": Kohl has never hesitated to invoke the danger that a Red/Green government would enact bold reforms that would hurt the German economy.

The *Verts* have clearly moved toward maximizing efficacy. A fusion of environmental and social demands has been paralleled by political fusion with the Center-Left and the Left. That strategy finally brought the *Verts* into the national parliament and government, demonstrating that they are not the marginal or sectarian force they once appeared to be. With their most prominent member holding two ministry posts, they have an impact on policy they could not have dreamed of earlier. Nevertheless, the new strategy fails to address the perennial source of danger to the *Verts'* identity: the French Socialist Party. The *Verts'* left-ecological strategy has placed them in the orbit of an entity that, once more, combines identity and efficacy to a remarkable degree. The new Socialist government rallies the Left and Center-left, as well as liberal and green currents. The *Verts* owe their new status to their negotiations with the PS, not to any political momentum of their own. Now the political vassals of the PS and Jospin, the *Verts* will stand or fall with the government they lead, but may have difficulty obtaining much of substance in return.

Combining identity and efficacy to the maximum degree, the new government should experience the maximum tensions associated with it. The Jospin administration must simultaneously represent alienation to hypercapitalism and maintain its commitment to the timetable for EMU. With a mandate for change and a diverse coalition demanding it, Jospin must nevertheless reassure France's European and American partners, plus the financial markets, of his basic moderation. The new Minister of the Environment herself must tread a difficult path. Dominique Voynet has to propose environmental change, yet do so as part of a government with close links to industry. If the leaders of the new government show political skill, they may stem popular disappointment with their actions. With the National Front already tapping into deep-seated public frustration with the political class, however, the prospect of disappointed hopes for change strikes an ominous tone for France, and not just for the *Verts* and their supporters.

Efficacy and Identity:
Applications to Green Politics and Beyond

The more oppositional parties like the *Verts* and the *Grünen* continue the process of expanding their base and become established in their political systems, the more they may tend to embrace diversity as an end in itself. This may be inherent in the move away from their original identity as the political arm of a grass-roots movement, and the corresponding move toward rallying a larger and wider group of citizens in elections and national-level politics. As their levels of support grow, their internal coalitions become more diverse. It is natural that they begin to elevate the defense of diversity, whether cultural, political, or national, to the level of a prior goal. Take for example the *Grünen's* argument that they were the voice of a rainbow coalition of social movements; or, for another, the *Verts'* ideal of cultural tolerance between extremely diverse, autonomous regions. The value on diversity is accompanied by emphasis on institutions that guarantee diversity and handle social complexity. The greens often advocate proportional representation, for example, or voting issue by issue in legislation. This sort of transformation occurred, for example, when West European communist parties entered their so-called Eurocommunist period during the 1970s. The more they acknowledged the complexity of the societies of which they were a part, and the range of progressive aims beyond those of the working class, the more they embraced parliamentarism and the prospect of a popular front with other progressive parties.

Yet it is possible that struggling for democratization or rights in the abstract—without framing them in terms of a partisanship of a certain aggrieved group—might represent a weak basis for party mobilization. Advocating the defense of liberal forms may bear a tactical advantage, where threatened by a clear adversary. But, given that the basic framework of democratic institutions already exists, individuals might otherwise not feel that action to support or improve them is worth the costs of political action. This was the case of nineteenth-century liberal parties, which are now tiny if they survive at all. The problem also held for the notion of Eurocommunism, since it meant that parties endorsing it moved closer in spirit and substance to the identities of social democratic parties, already wholly geared toward parliamentarism and electoralism. The embrace of pluralism and complexity that naturally follow from a strategy of efficacy in a given party organization or its support coalition poses another problem. The more intractable the centrifugal forces become, the more compelling is the logic of the charismatic leader who can command the support of each faction and guide the organization toward change. That logic has its own contradictions. The problems have been manifest in the case of the green realists like Fischer and especially Lalonde, who, preaching coalition, often practice obstructionism, as if to compensate for having undermined the need for their own independent leadership.

The greens may be moving in the direction of efficacy before they have fully constructed a clear identity. The tacit association between the greens and the Center-Left will continue: in the United States as much as Europe, it is assumed by the public and politicians alike that the environmental movement and the Democratic Party are natural allies. It is a matter of organizational surivival, then, that the ecologists build up their core base of support, and deepen it through closer organizational and ideological ties, before they reach out in alliances. The potential electoral support for environmentalism and related issues may add up, in theory, to as much as 15 percent of the vote in France and Northern Europe. The greens will have to work to consolidate this support by ending their internecine warfare, and addressing the left-wing, radical environmentalist, and liberal strains in this otherwise diverse group. Growing steadily as a force for opposition, they can then finally accede to government on their own terms.

The pure green identity may ultimately be the most viable basis on which to construct their own project for eventually governing. The *Grünen* have, after all, turned in the direction pioneered by the *Verts* during the period of the *Verts'* ascendancy between 1988 and 1993, and many European green parties are now pure green. That strategy succeeded in implanting the *Verts* despite the extremely unfavorable context in France, and they declined as soon as they abandoned it in the alliance with Brice Lalonde and GE in 1992 and 1993.

Yet there are also risks to confront in building an entire political identity around radical environmentalism. That assumes that there is an intense level of commitment to environmental issues among the greens' potential supporters, which is not yet the case. The issues involved are quite complex, especially when the social implications of environmental policies are factored in. Outside of a loose association with other-regarding ideals conveyed by green symbolism, the public still poorly understands how environmental fundamentals speak to social and political problems. As we saw, ecologists believe they have much to say on the subject. But they will have to explain these connections more effectively to win continued support. Above all, the environmental movement has to communicate the reasons why people should see nature itself as something of intrinsic value rather than an inconvenient necessity. This is the fundamental task in any strategy based on identity: one has to define how the values of the few speak to the interests of the many.

The problem of balancing the diverse interests of the many with the special needs of the few ranges beyond the politics of ecology or contemporary West European socialism. The dilemma may be framed as one of supporting representative institutions, which guarantee the expression of plural demands regardless of their content, versus addressing the demands of alienated groups with special or urgent claims to redress.[3] The issue of representation for all and redistribution for the weakest comes into play, for example, in the politics of European integration. European institutions may be more or less inclusive of new members and of the diverse demands all countries make on the European Union. Decisions by the European Council may require full consensus (giving a veto to each member), but the EU is moving in the direction of weighted majority voting (giving more influence to the larger countries). With Eastern European countries now applying for membership, current members are disputing the number of countries the EU can effectively sustain. These institutional questions have been complicated by economic ones. Poorer countries may not be able to trade on an equal footing, and more open institutions of course enable them to make their claims heard. But institutional issues may pit poor countries against each other as the EU widens and deepens. Prospective members (those of Central and Eastern Europe) will of course favor inclusiveness; and current members jealous of their voting rights and of the "competitive convergence funds" they already receive (especially large countries like Spain) may oppose it.

Within the postcommunist and postauthoritarian societies in Eastern Europe or Latin America, there is the problem of instituting democratic institutions in the first place, while also addressing the massive economic transformation the countries are undergoing. It is urgent that these societies address the needs of those buffetted by change (with welfare transfers to offset the effects of economic liberalization). It is equally vital to the new

democracies that citizens, regardless of class, enjoy political freedoms (through the institution of civil rights and parliamentary
representation). Yet acting on the two major goals at once might
destabilize the entire transition process.[4] In the more stable societies of the West, senior leaders are simultaneously dismantling
the welfare state, which underpinned a social and political consensus, and lamenting the public's disaffection with the political
process. The irony is exquisite in the matter of the xenophobic
parties of the far Right. The latter feed on their supporters' alienation from Europe-wide economic liberalization and its threat to
meaningful work and labor. Anti-immigrant parties seem to have
little commitment in principle to the democratic process whose
virtue it is to guarantee tolerance and representation for all. It
might not be too far-fetched to say that liberal institutions have to
be defended against a socially alienated group who might actually
have something to gain from them. The construction of Europe,
transitions to democracy, and the new nationalism bear more universal import than the concerns of political parties and their
strategies toward competitors. Yet parties may be expected to
take positions on different sides of these complex issues, and the
dynamics of competition between forces embracing efficacy and
those stressing identity will thus apply. In a world in flux, parties
will continually seek to redefine and refine the political blueprints
for reform and forge the coalitions and institutions around which
they can try to realize it. In the early twenty-first century, we can
hardly expect an end to ideology, but its redemption.

Notes

Chapter 1. Introduction: Competition and Change in Progressive Parties

1. Andrei Markovits and Phillip Gorski, *The German Left: Red, Green, and Beyond* (New York: Oxford, 1993); Helmut Wiesenthal, "Programme," *Die Grünen: Was sie wurden, was sie sind*, ed. Joachim Raschke (Koln: Bund-Verlag, 1992), 99–130.

2. On the French ecologists, see Guillaume Sainteny, *Les Verts*, Collection Encyclopédique, series # 2554 ("Que sais-je?"), ed. Paul Angoulvent (Paris: Presses Universitaires de France, 1991). For further discussion of ecosocialism and ecoanarchism, see Robyn Eckersley, *Environmentalism and Political Theory: Toward an Ecocentric Approach* (Albany: State University of New York Press, 1992).

3. From this point on, we use the term *environmentalism* to refer to any action to protect nature. *Ecology* or *political ecology*, on the other hand, refers to political initiatives, movements, parties, or ideas which are partly based on environmental themes, but which connect them to social and political issues and ideals.

4. Claus Offe, "The Attribution of Public Status to Interest Groups," *Disorganized Capitalism*, ed. John Keane (Cambridge, Mass.: MIT Press,

145

1985), 221–58; Suzanne Berger, "Politics and Anti-Politics in Western Europe," *Daedalus* 108.1 (1979): 27–48; Thomas Koelble, *The Left Unraveled: Social Democracy and the New Left Challenge in Britain and Germany* (Durham, N.C.: Duke University Press, 1991); Diane Parness, *The SPD and the Challenge of Mass Politics* (Boulder, Colo.: Westview, 1991).

5. Peter Katzenstein, *Policy and Politics in West Germany: The Growth of a Semi-Sovereign State* (Philadelphia: Temple University Press, 1987).

6. Robert Ladrech, "Social Movements and Party Systems: The French Socialist Party and New Social Movements," *West European Politics* 12.3 (1989): 262–79; Carl Boggs, *Social Movements and Political Power* (Philadelphia: Temple University Press, 1986); Steven Lewis and Serenella Sferza, "French Socialists between State and Society," *The Mitterrand Experiment*, eds. G. Ross, S. Hoffmann, and S. Malzacher (Cambridge, Mass.: Polity Press, 1987), 100–14.

7. This concept of a strategic tradeoff is strongly influenced by the work of Adam Przeworski, *Capitalism and Social Democracy* (Cambrigde, Mass.: Cambridge University Press, 1985); and Claus Offe and Helmut Wiesenthal, "Two Logics of Collective Action," in Offe, *Disorganized Capitalism*, ed. John Keane (Cambridge, Mass.: MIT Press, 1985), 170–220.

8. Przeworksi, *Capitalism and Social Democracy*, chs. 1 and 3.

9. Brendan Prendiville, *Environmental Politics in France* (Boulder, Colo.: Westview, 1994).

10. For a masterful survey of interpretations of nature found in these and other cultures, see Simon Schama, *Landscape and Memory* (New York: Alfred A. Knopf, 1995).

11. The literature on the relationship between ideas and political practice or political institutions is vast. See Max Weber, "Religious Rejections of the World and their Directions," *From Max Weber*, eds. H. H. Gerth and C. Wright Mills (New York: Oxford University Press, 1946), 323–62; Karl Mannheim, *Ideology and Utopia*, trans. Louis Wirth and Edward Shils (NewYork: Harcourt, Brace & World, 1936); Clifford Geertz, "Ideology as a Cultural System," *The Interpretation of Cultures*, ed. Geertz (New York: Basic Books, 1973), 193–233; and Peter Hall, ed., *The Political Power of Economic Ideas* (Princeton, N.J.: Princeton University Press, 1990).

12. Ronald Inglehart, *The Silent Revolution* (Princeton, N.J.: Princeton University Press, 1977).

13. Herbert Kitschelt, *The Logics of Party Formation: Ecological Politics in Belgium and West Germany* (Ithaca, N.Y.: Cornell University, 1989).

14. For summaries of this literature, see Jean Cohen and Andrew Arato, *Civil Society and Political Theory* (Cambridge, Mass.: MIT Press, 1992); and Barbara Epstein, "Rethinking Social Movement Theory," *Socialist Review* 90.1 (1990): 35–65.

15. The seminal work in this field is Giovanni Sartori, *Parties and Party Systems* (Cambridge, Mass.: Cambridge University Press, 1976).

Chapter 2. The Greens in Comparative Historical Perspective

1. Markovits and Gorski, *The German Left*; Koelble, *The Left Unraveled*; Diane Parness, *The SPD and the Challenge of Mass Politics*.

2. Albert Weale, "Vorsprung durch Technik? The Politics of German Environmental Regulation," *The Politics of German Regulation*, ed. K. Dyson (Aldershot, UK: Dartmouth, 1992), 159–183.

3. See Tony Chafer and Brian Jenkins, eds., *France: From the Cold War to the New World Order* (New York: St. Martin's, 1996).

4. On the history of the French environmental movement, see Prendiville, *Environmental Politics in France*; Kerry H. Whiteside, "The Resurgence of Ecological Thought in France," *French Politics and Society* 13.3 (1995): 43–58; and Roger Cans, "La France Écolo," *Le Monde* 10 June, 1992. On the institutional barriers to environmentalism in France, see Frank Wilson, "When Parties Refuse to Fail: The Case of France," *When Parties Fail*, ed. Kay Lawson (Princeton, N.J.: Princeton University Press, 1988), 503–32; Wilson, "Neo-Corporatism and the Rise of New Social Movements," *Challenging the Political Order: New Social and Political Movements in Western Democracies*, ed. Russell Dalton and Manfred Keuchler (New York: Oxford, 1990), 67–83; Herbert Kitschelt, "Political Opportunity Structures and Political Protest: Anti-nuclear Movements in Four Democracies," *British Journal of Political Science* 16.1 (1986): 57–85.

5. Claus Offe, "Reflections on the Welfare State and the Future of Socialism," interview, John Keane, in Offe, *Contradictions of the Welfare State* (Cambridge, Mass.: MIT Press, 1984).

6. Markovits and Gorksi, *The German Left*.

7. On Gaullism and its relationship to earlier patterns of administrative and executive power France, see J. E. S Hayward, *Governing France: The One and Indivisible Republic.* 2d ed. (New York: Norton, 1983). On the changes in the French party system under the Fifth Republic, see J. Charlot, "Le president et le partie majoritaire," *Revue politique et parlementaire* 905 (1983):27–42; and Olivier Duhamel, *La Gauche et la Cinquième République* (Paris: Presses Universitaires de France, 1980).

8. Our line of argument regarding the PS is indebted to Serenella Sferza, "The Shifting Advantages of Organizational Formats: Factionalism and the French Socialist Party," *The Mitterrand Era: Policy Alternatives and Political Mobilization in France*, ed. Anthony Daley (Basingstoke and New York: Macmillan, 1996), 189–205. Also see Herbert Kitschelt, *The Transformation of European Social Democracy* (Cambridge, Mass.: Cambridge University Press, 1994); Boggs, *Social Movements and Political Power.*

9. The PS's left wing was CERES (*Centre d'Études de Recherches et d'Éducation Socialistes*), and was headed by Jean-Pierre Chevènement. A *Mitterrandiste* current consisted of protegés of the party's leader, and reformists with a social democratic outlook who led powerful local federations, such as Pierre Mauroy or Gaston Defferre. The party's "Right," or liberal wing was headed by Michel Rocard and associates from the PSU.

10. Gerard Braunthal, *The German Social Democrats, 1969–82: Profile of a Party in Power*, 2d ed. (Boulder, Colo.: Westview, 1994).

11. On these factors in the PCF's decline, see George Ross, *Workers and Communists in France* (Berkeley: University of California Press, 1982).

12. On new middle-class support for the PS's initiatives, see Gerard Grunberg and Étienne Schweisguth, "Social Libertarianism and Economic Liberalism,"*The French Voter Decides*, ed. Daniel Boy and Nonna Mayer, trans. Cynthia Schoch (Ann Arbor: University of Michigan, 1993), 45–64. For a critique of the Auroux reforms, see Mark Kesselman, "French Labor Confronts Technological Change: Reform That Never Was?," *The Mitterrand Era,* 161–71.

13. The PS's numbers went from 61,000 to 146,000 between 1971 and 1974. SPD membership rose from 820,000 to 110, 000 between 1970 and 1972, hitting just a little over one million in 1976. Bell and Criddle, 200; Braunthal, 70.

14. Braunthal, 224.

15. Andrei Markovits, "West Germany's Political Future: The 1983 Bundestag Elections," *Socialist Review* 70 (1983): 83.

16. Lewis and Sferza, "French Socialists between State and Society."

17. See Julius Friend, "The PS Faces the 1990s," *French Politics and Society* 8.1 (1990) 14–24.

18. Only a small portion of the participants in the environmental or antinuclear movements played an active role in the green parties themselves. On the Federal Republic, see Werner Hulsberg, *The German Greens* (London: Verso, 1987), 78, 80. On France, Jean-Pierre Raffin, former president of the *Fédération des Societés pour la Protection de la Nature Française*, made this observation in a private interview.

19. On West Germany, see Hulsberg, *The German Greens*, 80; on France, see Guillaume Sainteny, "Les dirigeants écologistes et le champ politique." *Revue française de science politique* 37.1 (1987): 21–32.

20. Eugene Frankland and Donald Schoonmaker, *Between Protest and Power* (Boulder, Colo.: Westview, 1992), 85–86, 109.

21. Sainteny, *Les Verts*, 64–68; Jane Jenson, "From Babas Cool to a Vote Utile: The Trajectory of the French *Verts*," *French Politics and Society* 7.1 (1989): 1–15.

22. On the *Verts* experiment in governing the Nord/Pas-de-Calais regions, see Daniel Boy, Vincent-Jacques le Seigneur, and Agnès Roche, *L'écologie au pouvoir* (Paris: Presses de la Fondation des Sciences Politiques, 1995).

23. Daniel Boy, "Écologistes, les frères ennemis," *Le vote éclaté: les élections régionales et cantonales des 22 et 29 mars 1992*, ed. Pascal Perrineau, Phillipe Habert, and Collette Ysmal (Paris: Presses de la Fondation Nationale des Sciences Politiques, 1992), 209–30; Boy, *L'écologisme en France: évolutions et structures* (Paris: Cahiers de CEVIPOF, 1990); Boy, "Le vote écologiste en 1978," *Revue français de science politique*, 31.2 (April 1981): 394–416. Also see Jean-Luc Bennhamias and Agnès Roche, *Des Verts de toutes les couleurs: Histoire et sociologie du mouvement écolo*, (Paris: Albin Michel, 1992), ch. 3.1 "Lés electeurs écologistes," 167–68; Roche, "Mars 1993: une revelateur des faiblesses des écologistes," *Revue politique et parlementaire*, 964 (March–April 1993): 34–41; Hans-Joseph Veen and Jürgen Hoffmann, *Die Grünen zu Beginn der neunziger Jahre: Profil und Defizite einer fast tablierten Partei* (Bonn: Bouvier, 1992), ch. 7, "Wähler und Mitglieder," 92–118; and Frankland and Schoonmaker, *Between Protest and Power*, ch. 4, "The Greens and the Electorate," 67–85.

24. Veen and Hoffman, "Wähler und Mitgleider." The figure combines the categories of salaried employees and civil servants.

25. Boy, "Le vote écologiste en 1978."

26. Chafer, Tony. "The Greens in France: an Emerging Social Movement." *Journal of Area Studies* 10 (1984): 36–43.

27. Sainteny, *Les Verts*, ch. 4.1, "L' électorat," 77–90.

28. Roche, "Mars 1993: un revelateur."

29. Boy found that about 6 percent of the French green voters were in higher management; "le vote écologiste en 1978." In more recent data, Roche notes only 10–15 percent; "Mars 1993: une revelateur." With respect to West German ecological voters, Veen and Hoffmann find that 10–13 percent were higher civil servants from 1980 to 1990, and that only three to 6 percent were self-employed during the same time frame; Veen and Hoffmann, "Wähler und Mitgleider."

30. Veen and Hoffmann, "Wähler und Mitgleider."

31. Sainteny, "L'électorat."

32. Veen and Hoffmann, "Wähler und Mitgleider." These figures do include apprentices in manual trades.

33. With regard to supporters' levels of education, only the Centrists', with 36 percent, exceeded the *Verts*'; Bennhamias and Roche, *Des Verts* de toutes les couleurs.

34. Veen and Hoffman,"Wähler und Mitgleider."

35. Roche, "Mars 1993: un revelateur."

36. Sainteny, "L'électorat."

37. BVA/*Libération*, exit poll, March 21, 1993.

38. Boy "Frères ennemis"; Frankland and Schoonmaker.

39. Veen and Hoffman, "Wähler und Mitgleider."

40. Karl Cerny, ed. *Germany at the Polls: The Bundestag Elections of the 1980s* ("An American Enterprise Institute Book": published by Duke University Press, 1990), appendix B; table B.2.

41. Boy found that in 1978 only 38 percent of ecological voters chose a left-wing candidate on the second round, vs. 44 percent that came out for the right. Cf. Boy, "Évolutions et structures," on this shift toward leftist orientations.

42. Hulsberg, "Assessing the Greens;" Sainteny, "L'électorat."

43. Hulsberg, "Assessing the Greens"; Boy, "Le vote écologiste en 1978," Sainteny, "L'électorat."

44. Bennhamias and Roche, "Les électeurs écologistes."

45. Ibid.

46. Veen and Hoffmann, "Wähler und Mitgleider."

47. Ibid.

48. Jean-Luc Parodi, "Le nouvel espace politique français," *Ideologies, partis politiques et groupes sociaux*, ed. Yves Meny (Paris: Presses de la Fondation Nationale des Sciences Politiques, 1991), 49–60.

49. For example, negotiations between Lalonde (as a minister in the Rocard government) and the Ministry of Industry created the *Agence de l'Environnement et de la Maîtrise de l'Énergie* (ADEME) in 1991, fusing energy, waste disposal, and air quality authorities. In 1992, Lalonde succeeded in doubling the budget for water treatment to eighty-one billion francs over five years. Lalonde turned his attention to domestic policy, incidentally, only after the *Verts'* electoral sucesses of early 1989; he had previously concentrated on diplomacy and international issues (Jean-Pierre Raffin, private conversation, March 26, 1992). The Communist Party also tacitly acknowledged the *Verts'* popularity when they appointed marine biologist Sylvie Mayer to head its new section called "Environnement" in early 1991.

Chapter 3. Theoretical Considerations

1. Samuel Huntington, Michel Crozier, and Joji Watanuki, eds., *The Crisis of Democracy: Report to on the Government of Three Democracies to the Trilateral Commission* (New York: New York University Press, 1975).

2. Sartori's explicit concern with social cohesion and implicit criticism of the New Left reveal an unmistakeable accord with the overall precepts of the governability approach represented most by Huntington, Crozier et al.

3. Sartori, "The Sociology of Parties: A Critical Review," *Party Systems, Party Organizations, and the Politics of New Masses*, ed. Otto Stammer (Berlin: Institute for Political Science, Free University at Berlin, 1968), 1–25.

4. Jürgen Habermas, *Legitimation Crisis*, trans.T. McCarthy (Boston: Beacon, 1975).

5. Robert Michels, *Political Parties*, trans. Eden Paul and Cedar Paul (New York: Macmillan, 1962).

6. Maurice Duverger, *Political Parties: Their Organization and Activity in the Modern State*, 2d English ed., trans. Barbara North and Robert North (New York: Wiley, 1962), 215.

7. Anthony Downs, *An Economic Theory of Democracy* (New York: Harper and Row, 1957), ch. 6.

8. Downs, ch. 8; Duverger 407–408. Also see Alessandro Pizzorno, "Interests and Parties in Pluralism," *Organizing Interests in Western Europe*, ed. S. Berger (Cambridge, Mass.: Cambridge University Press, 1981), 249–86. Barring some astounding developments, we assume that all systems with a significant green party have three parties or more: there are simply no cases of party systems that comprise a green party and one other.

9. Downs 131–32.

10. Giovanni Sartori, *Parties and Party Systems*, ch. 6.

11. Sartori, *Parties and Party Systems*, 139–40.

12. Mark Kesselman and Joel Krieger, eds., *European Politics in Transition* (London: Heath, 1992).

13. Claus Offe, "Competitive Party Democracy and the Keynesian Welfare State," *Contradictions of the Welfare State* 170–206; Offe, "The Attribution of Public Status to Interest Groups," *Disorganized Capitalism*, ed. John Keane (Cambridge, Mass.: MIT Press, 1985), 221–58; Kitschelt, *The Logics of Party Formation*; Markovits and Gorski, *The German Left*.

14. Horst Kern and Michael Schumann, "New Concepts of Production in West German Plants," *Industry and Politics in West Germany: Toward the Third Republic*, ed. Peter Katzenstein (Ithaca, N.Y.: Cornell University Press, 1989), 87–112.

15. Kitschelt, *The Logic of Party Formation*, ch. 1.

16. M. F. Katzenstein and C. M. Mueller, "Introduction: Comparing the Feminist Movements of the United States and Western Europe," *The Women's Movement in the United States and Western Europe*, 3–22; Offe, "Competitive Party Democracy." Kitschelt suggests that the process of integrating these new issues along with promarket reforms should be rela-

tively easy for socialist parties; see Kitschelt, *Transformation of European Social Democracy* (Cambridge, Mass.: Cambridge University Press, 1994). He does not address the unfortunate results when the *Parti Socialiste*, now back on a leftist course, tried to do just that.

17. For an example of an earlier "relative deprivation" approach these writers wanted to revise, see Neil Smelser, *Theory of Collective Behavior* (New York: Free Press, 1962).

18. John D. McCarthy and Mayer N. Zald, "Resource Mobilization and Social Movements: A Partial Theory," *American Journal of Sociology* 82.6 (May 1977): 1212–41. For approaches that reflect more on the overall political processes, see Charles Tilly, "Parties," *From Mobilization to Revolution* (Ann Arbor: University of Michigan Press, 1977); and Sidney Tarrow, *Struggle, Politics and Reform: Social Movements, Protest, and Collective Action* (Ithaca, N.Y.: Cornell Center for International Studies,1989).

19. F. Piven and R. Cloward, *Poor Peoples' Movements: Why They Succeed, How They Fail* (New York: Random House, 1977).

20. McCarthy and Zald, "Resource Mobilization," 1216–17. On the potential of social movement networks for augmenting the capacity of individual movements, see Tarrow, *Struggle, Politics, and Reform.*

21. Tilly, *From Mobilization to Revolution.*

22. Tarrow, *Democracy and Disorder: Protest and Politics in Italy, 1965–1975* (Oxford: Clarendon, 1989).

23. Piven and Cloward, 27–34.

24. Kitschelt, *Logics of Party Formation*; Offe, "The Institutional Self-Transformation of New Social Movements"; Offe, "Challenging the Boundaries."

25. For an example, see Alberto Melucci, "New Movements, Terrorism, and the Political System: Reflections on the Italian Case," *Socialist Review* 56 (1981): 97–136; "The Symbolic Challenge of Contemporary Movements." *Social Research* 52. 4 (1985): 789–116.

26. Habermas, *Theory of Communicative Action*, trans. Thomas McCarthy. 2 vols. (Boston: Beacon Press, 1987), vol. 1, 75–101.

27. Alain Touraine, *The Voice and the Eye*, trans. Alan Duff (New York: Cambridge University Press, 1982), ch. 1. See also Jane Jenson, "From Party Formation to Paradigm Shift," paper presented to the American Political Science Association annual meeting, San Francisco, August, 1990; and William Gamson, "The Social Psychology of Collective Action," *Fron-*

tiers in Social Movement Theory, eds. Aldon Morris and Carol M. Mueller (New Haven, Conn.: Yale University Press, 1992), 53–76.

28. Touraine, *The Voice and The Eye*, 82.

29. Touraine, *Voice and the Eye*, 85.

30. Habermas, *Theory of Communicative Action*, vol. 2, 393.

31. Cohen and Arato, *Civil Society and Political Theory*, 511; Offe "Stage Model," 240.

32. Cohen and Arato, *Civil Society and Political Theory*.

33. For a discussion of the similar dilemmas in the workers' movement regarding parliamentary participation at the turn of the century, cf. Rosa Luxembourg, "The Mass Strike, the Political Party, and the Trade Unions," *Rosa Luxembourg Speaks*, ed. M. A. Waters (New York: Pathfinder, 1970), 153–218.

34. Jane Jenson, "From Party Formation to Paradigm Shift," 15.

35. Offe and Wiesenthal, "Two Logics," 179.

36. Offe and Wiesenthal, "Two Logics," 184.

37. Przeworski, *Capitalism and Social Democracy*, 105.

38. For a related approach, applied specifically to the German Greens, see Raschke, "Das Grüne Grundproblem," Raschke, *Die Grünen*, 33–36. The author notes a conflict between "legitimacy" and "efficiency"in the trajectory of the Greens.

39. Helmut Wiesenthal, *Realism in Green Politics*, ed. John Ferris. (Manchester, UK: Manchester University Press, 1993).

40. Wiesenthal, *Realism in Green Politics*.

41. This situation assumes, further, that the electoral system accords each party parliamentary representation in proportion to its level of support, such that there is no institutional incentive for an alliance or merger between the parties.

42. It might appear that we should make an exception in the case of the Left Party in Sweden. This party, however, shifted its profile in a new politics direction, so that it no longer resembles a typical West European Communist Party like the PCF.

43. Note that these games are analytically defined phases and do not necessarily correspond to single electoral contests. Chapters 6 through 9, the empirical portion of the book, correspond to them.

Chapter 4. Ideology and Competition
Inside Ecology Parties

1. Herbert Kitschelt, *The Logics of Party Formation*. See also Kitschelt, "Political Opportunity Structures and Political Protest: Anti-Nuclear Movements in Four Countries," *British Journal of Political Science* 16.1 (1986): 57–85. Kitschelt employs a similar framework in works on European socialist parties: Kitschelt, *The Transformation of European Social Democracy*.

2. Kitschelt, *Logics*, 1–5.

3. *Logics*, 274–75, 282. Cf. Jane Jenson, review of H. Kitschelt, *Logics of Party Formation*, *Comparative Political Studies* 25:1 (1992): 126–28.

4. Kitschelt groups ecology parties into the category of "left-libertarian" parties, which also includes reformed communist, democratic socialist, or New Left parties. Since his main cases are ecology parties—the German *Grünen* and the Belgian *Agalev* (Flemish) and *Ecolo* (Francophone)—we refer to them henceforth as "green parties" or "ecology parties."

5. Klaus von Beyme argues that internal party cleavages more often than not center on the actions of the "prevailing counterparty" rather than any fixed or prepolitical orientations of party activists. Von Beyme, *Political Parties in Western Democracies* (London: Gower, 1985).

6. Kitschelt, *Logics*, ch. 2.

7. Kitschelt, *Logics*, 50.

8. Kitschelt, *Logics*, 115–20.

9. Other literature notes not two but four major factional types within the German Greens. See Joachim Raschke, *Die Grünen: Wie sie wurden, was sie sind* (Koln: Bund-Verlag, 1992); Hans-Joachim Veen and Jurgen Hoffman, *Die Grünen: zu Beginn der neunziger Jahre* (Bonn: Bouvier, 1992); Werner Hulsberg, *The German Greens* (London: Verso, 1987); Gerd Langguth, *Der Grüne Faktor: von der Bewegung zur Partei?* (Osnabrück: Fromm, 1984).

10. Author Werner Hulsberg was once a *Grüne* activist and a member of the ecosocialist current. For a passage expressing this perspective, see Hulsberg, *The German Greens*, 77.

11. Kitschelt, *Logics*, 115.

12. Wolf-Dieter Hansenclever, Winfried Kretschmann, Ernst Hoplitshek, and Thomas Schmidt, "Ecolibertarian Manifesto," *Grüner Basis-Dienst* 3 (1984).

13. Veen and Hoffmann, *Die Grünen*, 70.

14. Veen and Hoffmann, *Die Grünen*, 61–63.

15. Cf. Robyn Eckersley, *Environmentalism and Political Theory* (Albany: State University of New York, 1992), ch. 5, on the ecosocialist core of the *Grüne* program. On the role of ecosocialists in the *Grünen*, see Markovits and Gorski, *The German Left*, 197; Vincent Hoffman-Martinot, "Two Faces of West European Ecologism," *West European Politics* 14. 4 (1991) 70–95; and Helmut Fogt, "The Greens and the New Left: Influences of Left Extremism on Green Party Organization and Policies,"*The Greens in West Germany*, ed. Eva Kolinsky (New York: St. Martin's, 1989), 89–121.

16. Cf. Raschke, *Die Grünen*; Hulsberg, *The German Greens*.

17. See Claus Offe, "New Social Movements: Challenging the Boundaries of Institutional Politics," *Social Research* 52.4 (1985): 817–68; and Langguth, *Der Grüne Faktor*.

18. *Le Monde*, 31 Aug., 1993.

19. *Le Monde*, 31 Aug., 1993. The epithet, which alluded to the Cambodian Khmer Rouge, was based on the notion that the *Verts* wanted to empty the cities and forcibly relocate the inhabitants to the countryside.

20. Cited in Frankland and Schoonmaker, *Between Protest and Power*, 105.

21. Markovits and Gorski, *The German Left*.

22. Quoted in Helmut Wiesenthal, *Realism in Green Politics*, ed. John Ferris (Manchester: Manchester University Press, 1992), 30.

23. Quoted in Hulsberg, *The German Greens*, 127.

24. Raymond Pronier and Vincent-Jacques le Seigneur, *Génération verte* (Paris: Presses de la Renaissance, 1992), ch. 5.

25. Jenson, "From Babas Cool to a Vote Utile." A. Roche notes that many of the *Verts* core voters were indeed also active in environmental groups; Bennhamias and Roche, *Des Verts des toutes les couleurs*.

26. Pronier and le Seigneur, *Génération verte*, 71.

27. Quoted in Pronier and le Seigneur, *Génération verte*, 104.

28. Andrei Markovits, "The West German Left in a Changing Europe: Between Intellectual Stagnation and Redefining Identity," *The Crisis of Socialism in Europe*, ed. Gary Marks and Christiane Lemke (Durham, N.C.: Duke, 1992), 171–90.

29. Hulsberg, *The German Greens*, 123.

30. Markovits and Gorski, *The German Left*, 130–42.

31. Pronier and le Seigneur, *Génération verte*, 294.

32. We use the term *dogmatic* to imply "holding unwavering principles." The aim is to distinguish these from more moderate ecosocialists.

33. Hulsberg, *The German Greens*, 128.

34. Entrons en Politique ("Let Us Enter Politics"), a strategy motion sponsored by Cochet at the *Verts'* 1987 *Assemblée Générale*.

35. Quoted in "Tout sur les écologistes," *Libération* special issue #9, Mar. 1993, p. 56.

36. Andrée Buchmann and Yves Cochet, Interview, *Deux Verts en politique*, by Jean-Louis Briquet, Guillaume Courty (Buchmann) and Jean-Baptiste Legavre (Cochet) *Politix* 9 (1991): 7–14.

37. Yves Cochet, "Écologie et démocratie," *Après-demain* 326 (1990): 17–26.

38. We shall discuss this aspect of Cochet's views in more detail when we examine his contribution to the *Verts'* programmatic documents in the next chapter.

39. Kitschelt, *Logics*, 48–62.

40. Kitschelt, *Logics*, 4–5, 62–68.

41. Kitschelt, *Logics*, chapter 9.

42. Kitschelt acknowledges that his analysis of the coalition "games" between greens and socialists does not incorporate the effect of reiterated games. Kitschelt, *Logics*, 268.

43. For a similar argument to the effect that green parties have little choice but to ally with the established Left, see Offe, "Challenging the Boundaries."

Chapter 5. Contrasting Images
of Ecological Politics

1. *Das Grüne Bundesprogramm* (Bonn: 1980); trans. Jonathon Poritt (London: Heretic, 1983) 8; *Les Verts et l'économie*, Alain Lipietz, dir. of publication (Paris:1992), 2.

2. Die Grünen, *Das Bundesprogram 1980* trans. Jonathon Poritt (London: Heretic, 1983) [henceforth *1980 Federal Program*] . . . *Sofortprogramm gegen Arbeitloskeit und Sozialabbau* ["Urgent Program against Unemployment and Declining Social Expenditures"] (Bonn: 1983) . . . *Umbau der Industriegesellschaft* ["Reconstruction of Industrial Society"] (Bonn:1986) in *The Greens in West Germany* (New York: St. Martin's, 1989), 252–57 [henceforth *Reconstruction Program*]; *1987 Federal Election Campaign Program*, in *The Greens in West Germany*, 253–54; Preamble to the *Grüne* Federal Party Constitution of 1987, *The Greens in West Germany* 243–44 . . . "Deutsch-Deutsch. Wider die Mauern auch in den eigenen Kopfen [Against the Walls in Each Head]," Die Grünen im Bundestag, Bonn, 1986; Kolinsky, *The Greens in West Germany* 244–49 . . . *Das Program zur 1. gesamtdeutschen Wahl* (Bonn:1990). Les Verts, *Les Verts et la nature* Guy Hascoët, dir. of publication (Paris, 1988) . . . *Les Verts et le tiers monde*, Hascoët, dir. of publication (Paris 1988); . . . *Les Verts et l'agriculture* (Paris:1988); . . . *Les Verts et la défense* Yves Cochet, dir. of pub. (Paris, 1988) . . . *Les Verts et l'éducation*, . . . *et la santé*, . . . *et les transports* Yves Cochet, dir. of pub. (Paris:1989); . . . *La choix de la vie* (Paris:1988, 1989); . . . *Les Verts et l'Europe* Yves Cochet, dir. of pub. (Paris:1989); . . . *Les Verts et l'économie* Alain Lipietz, dir. of pub. (Paris:1992); . . . *Les Verts et l'energie* Alain Fousseret, dir. of pub. (Paris 1990) . . . *Les Verts et les migrations: pour que les frontières tombent* Maguitte Dinguirard, dir of pub. (Paris:1992).

3. Radical and mainstream elements of the environmental movement both tend to advocate the decentralization of environmental policymaking. For an instance of the former, see Eckersley, *Environmentalism and Political Theory*. For the latter perspective, see Evan Ringquist, ed., *Environmental Protection at the State Level: Politics and Progress in Controlling Pollution* (Armonk, N.Y.: M. E. Sharpe, 1993).

4. Karl Marx, *On the Jewish Question*; *Capital* vol. 1.

5. *1980 Federal Program*, 10. Many of these views were reiterated and expanded in the *Reconstruction Program*.

6. *1980 Federal Program*, Section II.2.

7. *1980 Federal Program*, 48–50 ("Culture" and "Media", sections V.7 and V.8). Also see *Reconstruction Program*, 255.

8. *Reconstruction Program*, 254. For a classic statement of this view of the media's role in capitalism, and perhaps an indirect influence on the *Grünen*, cf. Theodore Adorno and Max Horkheimer, "The Culture Industry," *Dialectic of Enlightenment*, trans. J. Cumming (New York: Continuum, 1972), 120–67.

9. *1980 Federal Program*, 17, 50.

10. *Reconstruction Program*, 250–51.

11. For a discussion of these issues and their relationship to ecofeminism, see Eckersley, *Environmentalism and Political Theory*, 63–74.

12. *1980 Federal Program*, 39 (section V.2).

13. *Reconstruction Program*, 255.

14. *1980 Federal Program*, 11.

15. Cited in Frankland and Schoonmaker, *Between Protest and Power*, 132.

16. *Les Verts et l'économie*, 3.

17. *Les Verts et l'Europe*, 17.

18. *Les Verts et l'économie*, 5.

19. *Les Verts et l'économie*, 9.

20. *Les Verts et l'Europe*, 15.

21. *Les Verts et l'économie*, 3; *Les Verts et l'agriculture*, 2.

22. *1980 Federal Program*, 7.

23. Markovits and Gorski, *The German Left*, 167.

24. Claus Offe, "The Institutional Self-Transformation of the New Social Movements," 248–49.

25. *Reconstruction Program*, 255–56. The German ecologists drew some important activist and ideological support from a "self-help" movement milieu that reacted against the welfare bureaucracy. See Halfmann, "Social Mobilization and Political Change in West Germany."

26. As we noted in chapter 1, the German administrative system places strong authority at the level of the *Länder*. For this reason, the *Grünen* do not see the West German state as sufficiently decentralized, despite its federal structure.

27. *1980 Federal Program*, 8.

28. Marx's writings themselves are ambivalent about the source of and moral value of state power. The Communist Manifesto sees it as an instrument of bourgeois domination, whereas the *Eighteenth Brumaire of Louis Napoleon Bonaparte* suggests that, under certain conditions, the state may exercise power independently of any social class, including capital. The *Communist Manifesto* advocates the appropriation of state

power for the aim of achieving a classless society. *The Civil War in France* suggests a more radically democratic agenda. See David Held, *Models of Democracy* (Stanford, Calif.: Stanford University Press, 1987).

29. Frankland and Schoonmaker, *Between Protest and Power*, 130.

30. *Reconstruction Program*, 253, 256.

31. Quoted in Markovits and Gorski, *The German Left*, 173.

32. Cited in Frankland and Schoonmaker, *Between Protest and Power*, 136.

33. "Deutsch-Deutsch," 245.

34. "Deutsch-Deutsch," 245–49; Volker Grassnow, "The Greening of German-German Relations," *The Greens in West Germany*, ed. Kolinsky 141–58. On the attitudes of West German leftists toward the German Democratic Republic, see Andrei Markovits, "The West German Left in a Changing Europe: Between Intellectual Stagnation and Redefining Identity," *The Crisis of Socialism in Europe*, ed. Gary Marks and Christiane Lemke, 171–90.

35. Max Weber advanced a similar analysis of the state, though of course without drawing the same anarchist conclusion. Weber deliberately defined it in very abstract terms—i.e., as "the monopoly of legitimate coercion within a given territory"—leaving unspecified the political or social interests different states might serve. The state apparatus could be deployed for different aims in the specific types of rulership which lay at the core of Weber's political thought; i.e., traditional, bureaucratic/rational, or charismatic. Weber, "Political Communities," *Economy and Society*, ed. Roth and Wittich, vol. 2. (Berkeley: University of California Press, 1968) 901–40. On the relationship between internal and external state coercion, cf. Charles Tilly, "State-Making and War-Making as Organized Crime," *Bringing the State Back In*, ed. Peter Evans, Dietrich Reuschmeyer, and Theda Skocpol (Cambridge, Mass.: Cambridge University Press, 1985) 169–91. It is possible that the French state power could be interpreted in sheerly economic terms, and as derived from that of capital. Cf. the notion of Gaullism as "state monopoly capitalism" advanced by intellectuals of the *Parti Communiste Français* during the 1970s. See George Ross, *Workers and Communists in France* (Berkeley: University of California Press, 1982).

36. Antoine Waechter, *Dessine-moi une planète* (Paris: Albin Michel, 1990).

37. *Les Verts et l'énergie*, 1–2.

38. *Les Verts et l'Europe*, 31.

39. *Les Verts et l'économie*, 3.

40. *Les Verts et l'Europe*, 7–8,18; *Les Verts et le tiers monde*, 2–3; Cochet, "Écologie et démocratie."

41. *1980 Federal Program*, 27–29.

42. *1980 Federal Program*, 7.

43. *1980 Federal Program*, 10; *Reconstruction Program*, 253.

44. *Reconstruction Program*, 256.

45. A single chapter in the *1980 Federal Program*, "Individual and Society," covers questions of civil and political freedoms. These include freedom of conscience; political rights such as minority representation and openness and transparency in public policy; and the right to organize for strikes or demonstrations.

46. *1980 Federal Program*, 8–10.

47. *Reconstruction Program*, 253–54.

48. *1980 Federal Program*, 11–14; *Reconstruction Program*, 254–57.

49. *1980 Federal Program*, 10, 14.

50. *La choix de la vie*; *Les Verts et l'Europe*, 18. For a similar view of the benefits of participatory democracy, see Carol Pateman, *Participation and Democratic Theory* (Cambridge, Mass.: Cambridge University Press, 1970).

51. *Les Verts et l'Europe*, 23; Cochet, "Écologie et démocratie," 25.

52. Renée Conan, private interview, March 25, 1992.

53. Pierre Radanne, private interview, April 1, 1992, Paris.

54. *Les Verts et l'Europe*, 13, 18.

55. *Les Verts et l'Europe* 18; also see *Les Verts et l'éducation*, . . . *et les transports*, . . . *et l'agriculture*, . . . *et l'économie*.

56. *La choix de la vie*, 3; *Les Verts et l'Europe*, 22. *Les Verts et les migrations*, 7.

Chapter 6. Entering the Political Arena

1. Jutta Helm, "Citizen Lobbies in West Germany," *West European Party Systems: Trends and Prospects*, ed. Peter Merkl (New York: Free Press, 1980), 576–96.

2. Hulsberg, *The German Greens*, 91.

3. Hulsberg, *The German Greens*, 84–85.

4. Hulsberg, *The German Greens*, 84–93.

5. Hulsberg, *The German Greens*, 85.

6. See Eckersley, *Environmentalism and Political Theory* ch. 1.

7. Frankland and Schoonmaker, *Between Protest and Power*, 127–28.

8. Prendiville, *Environmental Politics in France*, 10–11.

9. Prendiville, *Environmental Politics in France*, 19–20.

10. MEP members Antoine Waechter, Solange Fernex, and Guy Cambot formed the core of the "pure ecological" current within the *Verts*, in the majority after 1986. Pronier and le Seigneur, *Génération verte*, 56; Sainteny, *Les Verts*, 18.

11. Braunthal, *The German Social Democrats*.

12. Parness, *The SPD and the Challenge of Mass Politics*.

13. Hulsberg, *The German Greens*, 64–65.

14. Frankland and Schoonmaker, *Between Protest and Power*, 127.

15. Y. Michal Bodemann, "The Green Party and the New Nationalism in the Federal Republic of Germany," *Socialist Register* (1985/86): 137–57; Hulsberg, *The German Greens*, 92–93.

16. James MacDonald, "Environmental Concerns and Local Political Inititiaves in France," *Geographic Record* 70.3 (1980): 343–49.

17. MacDonald, "Environmental Concerns and Local Political Initiatives in France," 343.

18. Kitschelt, "Political Opportunity Structures and Political Protest," 78.

19. MacDonald, "Environmental Initiatives and Local Political Concerns in France," 348.

20. Sainteny, *Les Verts*, 64–65.

21. Yves Cochet, "Political Ecology in France: 1974–1984," *Journal of Area Studies* 10 (1984): 45–46.

22. Bennhamias and Roche, *Des Verts de toutes les couleurs*, 66–71; Prendiville, *Environmental Politics in France*, 33.

23. Sainteny, *Les Verts*, 68.

24. Sainteny, *Les Verts*, 67.

Chapter 7. Defining Moments

1. Richard Löwenthal, "Identität und Zukunft der SPD," *Die Neue Gesellschaft* 28.12 (1981): 1085–89.

2. Markovits and Gorski, *The German Left*, 190; Boggs, *Social Movements and Political Power*, 188.

3. Markovits and Gorski, *The German Left*, 197.

4. Ferdinand Müller–Rommel, "The Social Democratic Party: The Campaigns and Electoral Outcomes of 1980 and 1983," *Germany at the Polls*, 88–110.

5. 79 percent of green voters at this point said they would choose Schmidt over Strauss if their vote would determine the chancellorship. Donald Schoonmaker, "The Greens and the Federal Elections of 1980 and 1983: Is the Opposition Waxing?" *Germany at the Polls*, 142–66.

6. Frankland and Schoonmaker, *Between Protest and Power*, ch. 6.

7. Cerny, *Germany at the Polls*, Appendix B. The second ballot determines the overall proportions of party representation in the *Bundestag*.

8. Müller-Rommel, "The SPD in 1980 and 1983," 106.

9. Markovits and Gorski, *The German Left*, 200–202

10. Parness, *The SPD and the Challenge of Mass Politics*.

11. See Boggs, *Social Movements and Political Power*, 188–89, Frankland and Schoonmaker, *Between Protest and Power*, 132–33.

12. Bell and Criddle, *The French Socialist Party*; Hayward, *Governing France*.

13. Grunberg and Schwiesguth, "Social Libertarianism and Economic Liberalism," 58–59.

14. Bell and Criddle, *The French Socialist Party*, 266. On the "liberal turn" in French politics during this period, see chapters by Jane Jenson "The French Left: A Tale of Two Beginnings," *Searching for the New France*, ed. George Ross and James Hollifield (New York: Routeledge, 1992), 85–112; George Ross, "Where Have All the Sartres Gone: The French Intelligentsia Born Again," *Searching for the New France*, 221–49; François Furet, Jacques Julliard, and Pierre Rosanvallon, *Le République du centre: fin de l'exception française* (Paris: Calman-Levy, 1988); Diana Pinto, "The Left, Intellectuals, and Culture," *The Mitterrand Experiment*, 217–28.

15. Jerome Jaffré and Olivier Duhamel, eds., *L'état de l'opinion français: clés pour 1988* (Paris: Seuil, 1988), notes that these items in its

platform drew new middle-class support for the PS during the period in question.

16. *Le Monde*, 9 Nov., 1984.

17. *Le Monde*, 13 Nov., 1985.

18. Ibid.

19. *Appel pour un Arc-en-Ciel*, text (January 1987).

20. O. Biffaud noted their "foggy" ["brouillé"] image in the eyes of the voters. *Le Monde*, 19–20 Nov., 1989.

21. *Le Monde*, 12 Nov., 1986.

22. *Le Monde*, 9 Nov., 1986.

23. *Le Monde*, 9 Nov., 1986.

24. Pronier and le Seigneur, *Génération verte*, 127.

25. *Le Monde*, 12 Nov., 1986.

26. *Le Monde*, 9 Nov., 1986; 6 Aug., 1988.

27. Interview, *Le Monde*, 6 Aug., 1988.

28. *Reuters*, 14 Mar., 1989.

29. For further discussion of the *Verts'* new emphasis on strict questions of the environment at this point, see Sainteny, *Les Verts*, 69.

30. The German Greens received reimbursement through campaign expenditures from state funds at a much earlier point, i.e., in 1980, due to lower thresholds and other different criteria. See Jenson, "From Babas Cool to a Vote Utile."

31. Sainteny, *Les Verts*, 91.

32. Bennhamias and Roche, *Des Verts de toutes les couleurs*, 81; Jenson, "From Babas Cool to a Vote Utile."

Chapter 8. Consolidation—and New Tensions

1. Parness, *The SPD and the Challenge of Mass Politics*, 162; Markovits and Gorski, *The German Left*, 223.

2. Parness, *The SPD and the Challenge of Mass Politics*, 153, 173n.

3. Markovits and Gorski, *The German Left*, 231.

4. Markovits and Gorski, *The German Left*, 210.

5. Markovits and Gorski, *The German Left*, 202.

6. Markovits and Gorski, *The German Left*, 213–14.

7. Prendiville, *Environmental Politics in France*, 48–49.

8. See our analysis of vote transfers between the *Verts* and the PS in chapter 2.

9. "Écologie: une philosophie de partage,"*Tribune des Verts: Special Assemblée Générale / Strasbourg*, Nov. 1990, p. 15. In 1989, as a deputy to the European Parliament, Waechter had abstained from voting on the lifting of parliamentary immunity for FN head Jean-Marie Le Pen for antisemitic remarks. Waechter held that that bestowed Le Pen with the aura of a persecuted victim; Pronier and Seigneur, *Génération verte*, 198.

10. *Tribune des Verts: Special Assemblée Générale / Strasbourg*, 12.

11. *La Croix de l'Òvénement*, 16 Nov., 1990; *Libération*, 9–10 Nov., 1991.

12. *Tribune des Verts: Special AG St-Brieuc*, 12.

13. Brière referred to Israel with the word *belligène*, a neologism with a deliberately biological connotation.

14. Brière, already known for his pungent opinions, was a member of the left-ecological current. It would be spurious to link his views with the Waechterians, their pure ecological program, or their effort to distance themselves from the Left, though the press occasionally did so. For a throrough account of this episode, see Pronier and Seigneur, *Génération verte*, ch. 8.

15. Pronier and Seigneur, *Génération verte*, 245.

16. Pronier and Seigneur, *Génération verte*, 253–260.

17. For example, Phillipe Reinhaud, "Le rouge est dans le fruit," *Le Quotidien*, 7 Oct., 1991.

18. BVA/*Libération* survey, 10 Feb, 1992 ("Tout sur les écologistes," 47–50).

19. Boy, "Frères ennemis."

20. Of the PS list's voters in the 1989 European Parliament elections, *GE* gained 8 percent, according to SOFRES, 9 percent for BVA, 9 percent for IFOP; exit polls in March, 1992. From the Centrist list in 1989, it

gained 7 percent, 8 percent, or 12 percent according to the same organizations, respectively; Boy, "Frères ennemis."

21. Daniel Boy, "Les écologistes en France."

Chapter 9. Cataclysm and Renewal

1. Markovits, "The West German Left in a Changing Europe."

2. Braunthal, 206.

3. Frankland and Schoonmaker, *Between Protest and Power*, 142–143.

4. Prendiville, *Environmental Politics in France*, 60.

5. *Financial Times*, 23 May, 1995.

6. Daniel Cohn-Bendit, interview, *Reuter Textline/Agence Europe* ("European Union: Texts of the Week"), 10 May, 1997.

7. Chirac's term of office, however, does not expire until the year 2002.

8. Ecologist seats include those of CES and AREV. Waechter's and Lalonde's organizations (i.e., the MEI and GE, respectively) were eliminated in the first round.

9. Dick Richardson and Chris Rootes, eds., *The Green Challenge: the Development of Green Parties in Europe* (London: Routledge, 1995); Herbert Kitschelt, *The Transformation of European Social Democracy*; Ferdinand Müller-Rommel, ed., *New Politics in Western Europe* (Boulder, Colo.: Westview, 1989).

10. Wolfgang Rudig and P. D Lowe, "The Withered Greening of British Politics: A Study of the Ecology Party," *Political Studies* 34 (1986): 262–84.

11. They scored 0.7 percent in 1974, having run four candidates; 1.5 percent in 1979, with fifty-three candidates, and 2.6 percent in 1984 in the sixteen divisions where they participated.

12. Dick Richardson, "The Green Challenge: Philosophical, Programmatic, and Electoral Considerations," *The Green Challenge*, 4–22.

13. Chris Rootes, "Britain: the Greens in a Cold Climate," *The Green Challenge*, 66–90.

14. Christian Haerpfer, "Austria: The 'United Greens' and the 'Alternative List/Green Alternative'," *New Politics*, 23–38.

15. Kitschelt, *The Transformation of European Social Democracy*, 189–91.

16. In fact, *Ecolo* has resisted the temptation to act as a pivot party, despite the role that Belgium's party system, which tends to favor coalition, might have accorded them. They refused an offer from the PRL, the center-right Walloon Liberal Party, to change their working parliamentary alliance with the Socialists.

17. In the Flemish portion, the situation has been complicated by the arrival of the populist and antipolitical *Rossem* party, which absorbed some protest votes from the Flemish Green Party, *Agalev*. Thus their vote dropped from 10 percent to 7 percent in 1991.

18. Kitschelt, *Transformation*, 240–41.

19. De Groenen scored 1.3 percent in the 1984 European Parliament elections; 0.2 percent in the 1986 National Parliament elections; and 0.4 percent in the 1989 Europeans.

20. Gerrit Voerman, "The Netherlands: Losing Colours, Turning Green," *The Green Challenge*, 109–27.

21. Martin Rhodes, "Italy: the Greens in an Overcrowded Political System," *The Green Challenge*, 168–92.

22. "Ennesimo partitino della sinistra"; quoted in Rhodes, "Italy," 184.

Chapter 10. Conclusion

1. In fact, it is possible that relatively hierarchic forms of party organization do not necessarily contradict the goal of winning progressive reforms for a broader constituency outside the party. Cf. Max Weber, "The Realities of Party Politics and the Fallacy of the Corporate State," *Economy and Society*, vol. 2, 1395–99 and "The Impact of Democratization on Party Organization and Leadership," *Economy and Society*, vol. 2, 1443–49. Further work might examine the relationship between the level of internal democracy in green parties and their external efficacy in policy or in politics.

2. *Financial Times*, 10 Oct., 1995.

3. Tsebelis discusses the competing rationalities of "efficient" versus "redistributive" institutions: the former improve the conditions of all individuals or groups in a society; the latter improve those of one group at

the expense of another. Cf. George Tsebelis, *Nested Games: Rational Choice in Comparative Politics* (Berkeley: University of California Press, 1990) 104. Democratic theorists have debated the relative merits of procedural versus substantive conceptions of democracy. See Carol Pateman, *Participation and Democratic Theory* (Cambridge, Mass.: Cambridge University Press, 1970); Isaiah Berlin, *Four Essays on Liberty* (Oxford: New York, 1979); and Held, *Models of Democracy*.

4. See Adam Przeworski, *Democracy and the Market: Political and Economic Reforms in Eastern Europe and Latin America* (Cambridge, Mass.: Cambridge University Press, 1991); Guillermo O'Donnell, Phillipe Schmitter, and Lawrence Whitehead, eds., *Transitions from Authoritarian Rule*, 4 vols. (Baltimore: Johns Hopkins University Press, 1986).

Selected Bibliography

Adorno, Theodore, and Max Horkheimer. "The Culture Industry: Enlightenment as Mass Deception." *Dialectic of Enlightenment.* Trans. John Cumming. New York: Continuum, 1986. 120–67.

Bahro, Rudolph. *From Red to Green: Interviews in New Left Review.* Trans. Gus Fagan and Richard Hurst. London: Verso, 1984.

Belden Fields, A. *Trotskyism and Maoism: Theory and Practice in France and the United States.* New York: Praeger, 1989.

Bell, Daniel. *The Coming of Post-Industrial Society: A Venture in Social Forecasting.* New York: Basic Books, 1973.

Bell, D. S., and Byron Criddle. *The French Socialist Party.* Oxford: Clarendon, 1988.

Bennhamias, Jean-Luc, and Agnès Roche. *Des Verts de toutes les couleurs: histoire et sociologie du mouvement écolo.* Paris: Albin Michel, 1992.

Berger, Suzanne, ed. *Organizing Interests in Western Europe: Pluralism,Corporatism, and the Transformation of Politics.* Cambridge, Mass.: Cambridge University Press, 1981.

———. "Politics and Anti-Politics in Western Europe in the Seventies." *Daedalus* 108.1 (1979): 27–48.

Berlin, Isaiah. *Four Essays on Liberty.* Oxford: New York, 1979.

Beyme, Klaus von. *Political Parties in Western Democracies.* London: Gower, 1985.

Bodemann, Y. Michal. "The Green Party and the New Nationalism in the Federal Republic of Germany." *Socialist Register* (1985/86): 137–57.

Bollafi, Angelo, and Otto Kallshauer. "Die Grünen: Farbenlehre eines Politiches Paradoxes. Zwischen neuen Bewegungen und Veränderung der Politik." *Prokla* 51 (1983): 62–105.

Boggs, Carl. *Social Movements and Political Power*. Philadelphia: Temple University Press, 1986.

Boy, Daniel. "Les écologistes en France." *French Politics and Society* 10.3 (1992): 1–25.

———. *L'écologisme en France: évolutions et structures*. Paris: Cahiers de CEVIPOF, 1990.

———. "Le vote écologiste en 1978." *Revue française de science politique* 31.2 (1981): 394–416.

Boy, Daniel, Vincent-Jacques le Seigneur, and Agnès Roche. *L'écologie au pouvoir*. Paris: Presses de la Fondation des Sciences Politiques, 1995.

Boy, Daniel, and Nonna Mayer, eds. *The French Voter Decides*. Trans. Cynthia Schoch. Ann Arbor: University of Michigan Press, 1993.

Boy, Daniel, Agnès Roche, and Anne Muxel. "Jeunes écologistes: un portrait en creux." Habert, Perrineau, and Ysmal, *Le vote sanction* 267–87.

Braunthal, Gerard. *The German Social Democrats, 1969–82: Profile of a Party in Power*. 2d ed. Boulder, Colo.: Westview, 1994.

Buchmann, Andreé, and Yves Cochet. Interview. *Deux Verts en politique*. By Jean-Louis Briquet, Guillaume Courty (Buchmann), and Jean-Baptiste Legavre (Cochet). *Politix* 9 (1991): 7–14.

Capdevieille, Jacques, and René Mouriaux. *Mai '68: l'entredeux de la modernité*. Paris: Presses de la Fondation Nationale des Sciences Politiques, 1988.

Cerny, Karl, ed. *Germany at the Polls: The Bundestag Elections of the 1980s*. Durham, N.C.: Duke University Press, 1990.

Cerny, Phillip, and Martin Schain, eds. *French Politics and Public Policy*. London: Methuen, 1980.

Chafer, Tony, and Brian Jenkins, eds. *France: From the Cold War to the New World Order*. New York: St. Martin's, 1996.

———. "The Greens in France: An Emerging Social Movement." *Journal of Area Studies* 10 (1984): 36–43.

Charlot, Jean. "Le président et le partie majoritaire." *Revue politique et parlementaire* 905 (1983): 27–42.

Cochet, Yves. "Écologie et démocratie." *Après-demain* 326 (1990): 18–25.

———. "Political Ecology in France: 1974–1984." *Journal of Area Studies* 10 (1984): 45–46.

Cohen, Jean, and Andrew Arato. *Civil Society and Political Theory*. Cambridge, Mass.: MIT, 1992.

Crewe, Ivor, and David Denver, eds. *Electoral Change in Western Democracies: Patterns and Sources of Electoral Volatility*. London: Croom Helm, 1985.

Daley, Anthony, ed. *The Mitterrand Era: Policy Alternatives and Political Mobilization in France*. Basingstoke and New York: Macmillan and NYU Press, 1996.

Dalton, Russell J. *The Green Rainbow: Environmental Groups in Western Europe*. New Haven, Conn.: Yale University Press, 1994. 37–45.

Dalton, Russell J., and Manfred Keuchler. *Challenging the Political Order: New Social and Political Movements in Western Democracies*. New York: Oxford, 1990.

Dalton, Russell J., Scott Flanagan, and P. A. Beck, eds. *Electoral Change in Advanced Industrial Societies: Realignment or Dealignment?* Princeton, N.J.: Princeton University Press, 1984.

Dalton, Russell J., and Scott Flanagan. "Parties under Stress: Realignment or Dealignment in Advanced Industrial Societies?" *West European Politics* 7.1 (1984): 7–23.

Downs, Anthony. *An Economic Theory of Democracy*. New York: Harper and Row, 1957.

Duhamel, Olivier. *La Gauche et la Ve République*. Paris: Presses Universitaires de France, 1980.

Duverger, Maurice. *Political Parties: Their Organization and Activity in the Modern State*. 2d English ed. Trans. Barbara North and Robert North. New York: Wiley, 1963.

Dyson, Kenneth, ed. *The Politics of German Regulation*. Brookfield, Vt.: Dartmouth, 1992.

Eckersley, Robyn. *Environmentalism and Political Theory: Toward an Ecocentric Approach*. Albany: State University of New York Press, 1992.

Epstein, Barbara. "Rethinking Social Movement Theory." *Socialist Review* 90.1 (1990): 35–65.

Esping-Anderson, Gosta. *Politics against Markets*. Princeton, N.J.: Princeton University Press, 1985.

Evans, Peter, Theda Skocpol, and Dietrich Reuschmeyer, eds. *Bringing the State Back In*. Cambridge, Mass.: Cambridge University Press, 1984.

Favier, Pierre, and Michel Martin-Roland. *La Décennie Mitterrand*, 2 vols. Paris: Seuil, 1990.

Ferry, Luc. *Le nouvel ordre écologique*. Paris: Grasset, 1992.

Frankland, Eugene, and Donald Schoonmaker. *Between Protest and Power: The Green Party in Germany*. Boulder, Colo.: Westview, 1992.

Friend, Julius. "The PS Faces the 1990s." *French Politics and Society* 8.1 (1990): 14–24.

Furet, François, Jacques Julliard, and Pierre Rosanvallon. *Le République du centre: fin de l'exception française*. Paris: Calman-Levy, 1988.

Geertz, Clifford. *The Interpretation of Cultures*. New York: Basic Books, 1973.

Giddens, Anthony. *Studies in Social and Political Theory*. New York: Basic Books, 1977.

Gorz, Andre. *Farewell to the Proletariat: An Essay on Post-Industrial Socialism*. Trans. M. Sonenstein. Boston: South End, 1982.

Gouldner, Alvin. *The Future of Intellectuals and the Rise of the New Class*. New York: Seabury, 1979.

Die Grünen. *Das Program zur 1. gesamtdeutschen Wahl*. Bonn, 1990.

———. *Bundestagswahlprogram 1987*. Bonn, 1987.

———. *Satzung der Bundespartei Die Grünen*. Bonn, 1987

———. *Deutsch-Deutsch. Wider die Mauern auch in den eigenen Köpfen*. Bonn, 1986.

———. *Umbau der Industriegesellschaft*. Bonn,1986.

———. *Grüne Parliamentary Group Report*. Bonn, 1984.

———. *Sofortprogramm gegen Arbeitloskeit und Sozialabbau*. Bonn, 1983.

———. *Das Bundesprogram 1980*. Bonn, 1980.

Habermas, Jürgen. *Theory of Communicative Action*. Trans. Thomas McCarthy. 2 vols. Boston: Beacon Press, 1987.

———. *Legitimation Crisis*. Trans. Thomas McCarthy. Boston: Beacon, 1975.

———. *Toward a Rational Society*. Trans. J. Shapiro. Boston: Beacon: 1970.

Habert, Phillipe, Pascal Perrineau, and Collette Ysmal, eds. *Le vote sanction: les élections législatives des 21 et 28 Mars 1993*. Paris: Presses de la Fondation des Sciences Politiques, 1993.

———. *Le vote éclate: les élections régionales et cantonales des 22 et 29 Mars 1992*. Paris: Presses de la Fondation Nationale des Sciences Politiques, 1992.

Hall, Peter. *The Political Power of Economic Ideas: Keynesianism across Nations*. Princeton, N.J.: Princeton University Press, 1990.

Hauss, Charles. *The New Left in France: The Unified Socialist Party*. Westport, Conn.: Greenwood, 1978.

Hayward, J. E. S. *Governing France: The One and Indivisible Republic*. 2d ed. New York: Norton, 1983.

Held, David. *Models of Democracy*. Stanford, Calif.: Stanford University Press, 1987.

Hoffman Martinot, Vincent. *"Grüne* and *Vert*: Two Faces of European Ecologism." *West European Politics* 14.4 (1991): 70–95.

Huelshoff, M. G., Andre Markovits, and Simon Reich, eds. *From Bundesrpublik to Deutschland: German Politics after Unification.* Ann Arbor: University of Michigan Press, 1993.

Hüllen, Rudolph van. *Ideologie und Machtkampf bei den Grünen.* Bonn: Bouvier, 1990.

Hulsberg, Werner. *The German Greens.* London: Verso, 1988.

Huntington, Samuel, Michel Crozier, and Joji Watanuki. *The Crisis of Democracy: Report on the Government of Three Democracies to the Trilateral Commission.* New York: New York University Press, 1975.

Illich, Ivan. *Tools for Conviviality.* New York: Harper and Row, 1973.

Inglehart, Ronald, and Paul R. Abramsom. "Economic Security and Value Change." *American Political Science Review* 88.2 (1994): 336–54.

———. *Culture Shift in Advanced Industrial Societies.* Princeton, N.J.: Princeton University Press, 1990.

———. *The Silent Revolution.* Princeton, N.J.: Princeton University Press, 1977.

———. "The Silent Revolution in Europe: Intergenerational Change in Postindustrial Societies." *American Political Science Review* 65 (1971): 991–1017.

Jaffré, Jerome, and Olivier Duhamel, eds. *L'état de l'opinion Français: clés pour 1988.* Paris: Seuil, 1988.

Jenson, Jane. "The French Left: A Tale of Two Beginnings." Ross and Hollifield, *Searching for the New France,* 85–112

———. rev. of *The Logics of Party Formation, Comparative Political Studies* 25:1 (1992): 126–28.

———. "From Party Formation to Paradigm Shift: The Experience of the French Greens." Paper presented to the American Political Science Association annual meeting, San Francisco, August, 1990.

———. "From Babas Cool to a Vote Utile: The Trajectory of the French Verts." *French Politics and Society* 7.4 (1989): 1–15.

Katsiaficas, George. *The Imagination of the New Left: A Global Analysis of 1968.* Boston: South End, 1987.

Katzenstein, Mary Fainsod, and Carol M. Mueller, eds. *The Women's Movements of the United States and Europe.* Philadelphia: Temple University Press, 1987.

Katzenstein, Peter. *Industry and Politics in West Germany: Toward the Third Republic.* Ithaca, N.Y.: Cornell, 1989.

———. *Policy and Politics in West Germany: The Growth of a Semi-Sovereign State.* Philadelphia: Temple University Press, 1987.

Katznelson, Ira, and Aristide Zolberg, eds. *Working Class Formation*. Princeton, N.J.: Princeton University Press, 1986.

Kesselman, Mark. "Lyrical Illusions or a Socialism of Governance: Whither French Socialism." *Socialist Register* (1985/86): 233–47.

Kitschelt, Herbert. *The Transformation of European Social Democracy*. Cambridge, Mass.: Cambridge University Press, 1994.

———. "La gauche libertaire et les écologistes franais." *Revue française de science politique* 40.3 (1990): 339–65.

———. *The Logics of Party Formation: Ecological Politics in Belgium and West Germany*. Ithaca, N.Y.: Cornell, 1989.

———. "Political Opportunity Structures and Political Protest: Anti-nuclear Movements in Four Democracies." *British Journal of Political Science* 16.1 (1986): 57–85.

Koelble, Thomas. *The Left Unraveled: Social Democracy and the New Left Challenge in Britain and Germany*. Durham, N.C.: Duke University Press, 1991.

Kolinsky, Eva, ed. *The Greens in West Germany*. New York: St. Martin's, 1989.

Laclau, Ernesto, and Chantal Mouffe. *Hegemony and Socialist Strategy: Toward a Social Democratic Politics*. London: Verso, 1985.

Ladrech, Robert. "Social Movements and Party Systems: The French Socialist Party and New Social Movements." *West European Politics* 12.3 (1989): 262–79.

Langguth, Gerd. *Der Grüne Faktor. Von der Bewegung zur Partei?* Osnabrück: Fromm, 1984.

La Palombara, Joseph, and Myron Weiner, eds. *Political Parties and Political Development*. Princeton, N.J.: Princeton University Press, 1966. 177–200.

Lawson, Kay, ed. *When Parties Fail*. Princeton, N.J.: Princeton University Press, 1988.

Leaman, Jeremy. *The Political Economy of West Germany:1948–1985*. London: Macmillan, 1988.

Lipietz, Alain. *Vert espérance: L'avenir de l'écologie politique*. Paris: Decouverte, 1990.

Lipset, S. M., and Stein Rokkan, eds. *Party Systems and Voter Alignments*. New York: Free Press, 1967.

Löwenthal, Richard. "Identität und Zukunft der SPD." *Die Neue Gesellschaft* 28.12 (1981): 1085–89.

MacDonald, James. "Environmental Concerns and Local Political Initiatiaves in France." *Geographic Record* 70.3 (1980): 343–49.

Mannheim, Karl. *Ideology and Utopia*. Trans. Louis Wirth and Edward Shils. NewYork: Harcourt, Brace and World, 1936.

Marcuse, Herbert. *One Dimensional Man: Studies in the Ideology of Advanced Industrial Societies*. London: Routeledge and Kegan Paul, 1964.

Markovits, Andrei, and Phillip Gorski. *The German Left: Red, Green, and Beyond*. New York: Oxford, 1993.

———. "West Germany's Political Future: The 1983 Bundestag Elections." *Socialist Review* 70 (1983): 67–98.

———. *The Political Economy of West Germany: Modell Deutschland*. New York: Praeger, 1982.

Marks, Gary, and Christiane Lemke. *The Crisis of Socialism in Europe*. Durham, N.C.: Duke University Press, 1992.

Marx, Karl. *The Civil War in France*. London, 1871.

———. *Capital* vol. 1. London, 1867.

———. *The Eighteenth Brumaire of Louis Napoleon Bonaparte*. London, 1852.

———. *Communist Manifesto*. London, 1848.

———. *On the Jewish Question*. Paris, 1848.

McCarthy, John D., and Mayer N. Zald. "Resource Mobilization and Social Movements: A Partial Theory." *American Journal of Sociology* 82.6 (May 1977): 1212–41.

McCarthy, Patrick, ed. *The French Socialists in Power, 1981–1986*. Westport, Conn.: Greenwood, 1987.

Melucci, Alberto. "New Movements, Terrorism, and the Political System: Reflections on the Italian Case." *Socialist Review* 56 (1981): 97–136

———. "The Symbolic Challenge of Contemporary Movements." *Social Research* 52. 4 (1985): 789–816.

Meny, Yves, ed. *Idéologies, partis politiques et groupes sociaux*. Paris: Presses de la Fondation Nationale des Sciences Politiques, 1991.

Merkl, Peter. *West European Party Systems: Trends and Prospects*. New York: Free Press, 1980.

Michels, Robert. *Political Parties*. Trans. Eden Paul and Cedar Paul. New York: Macmillan, 1962.

Morris, Aldon, and Carol McClurg Mueller, eds. *Frontiers in Social Movement Theory*. New Haven, Conn.: Yale University Press, 1992.

Müller-Rommel, Ferdinand. *New Politics in Western Europe*. Boulder, Colo.: Westview, 1989.

Nelkin, Dorothy and Michael Pollak. *The Atom Beseiged: Antinuclear Movements in France and Germany*. Cambridge, Mass.: MIT Press, 1981.

O'Donnell, Guillermo, Phillipe Schmitter, and Lawrence Whitehead, eds. *Transitions from Authoritarian Rule*. 4 vols. Baltimore: Johns Hopkins University Press, 1986.

Offe, Claus. *Disorganized Capitalism*. ed. John Keane. Cambridge, Mass.: MIT Press, 1985.

———. "New Social Movements: Challenging the Boundaries of Institutional Politics." *Social Research* 52.4 (1985): 817–68. (cf Meluci citation)

———. *Contradictions of the Welfare State*. Ed. John Keane. Cambridge, Mass.: MIT Press, 1984.

———. "Structural Problems in the Capitalist State." *German Political Studies* 1 (1974): 31–58.

Oppeln, Sabine von. "Politique de l'environnement: comparison entre RFA et RDA et la France." *Allemagne aujourd'hui* 109–110 (1989): 243–58.

Padgett, Stephen, and Tony Burkett. *Political Parties in West Germany: The Search for a New Stability*. New York: St. Martin's, 1986.

Parness, Diane. *The SPD and the Challenge of Mass Politics*. Boulder, Colo.: Westview, 1991.

Parodi, Jean-Luc. *La Cinquième République et le système majoritaire*. Paris: Presses Universitaires de France, 1973.

Pateman, Carol. *Participation and Democratic Theory*. Cambridge, Mass.: Cambridge University Press, 1970.

Piven, Frances Fox, and Richard A Cloward. *Poor Peoples' Movements: Why They Succeed, How They Fail*. New York: Random House, 1977.

Prendiville, Brendan. *Environmental Politics in France*. Boulder, Colo.: Westview, 1994.

Pronier, Raymond, and Vincent-Jacques le Seigneur. *Génération verte*. Paris: Presses de la Renaissance, 1992.

Przeworski, Adam, and John Sprague. *Paper Stones: A History of Electoral Socialism*. Chicago: University of Chicago Press, 1986.

Przeworski, Adam. *Democracy and the Market: Political and Economic Reforms in Eastern Europe and Latin America*. Cambridge, Mass.: Cambridge University Press, 1991.

———. *Capitalism and Social Democracy*. Cambridge, Mass.: Cambridge University Press, 1985.

Raschke, Joachim, ed. *Die Grunen: Was sie wurden, was sie sind*. Köln: Bund-Verlag, 1993.

Richardson, Dick, and Chris Rootes, eds. *The Green Challenge: The Development of Green Parties in Europe*. London: Routledge, 1995.

Ringquist, Evan, ed. *Environmental Protection at the State Level: Politics and Progress in Controlling Pollution*. Armonk, N.Y.: M. E. Sharpe, 1993.

Roche, Agnès. "Mars 1993: une révélateur des faiblesses des écologistes." *Revue politique et parlementaire* 964 (1993): 34–41.

Ross, George, and James Hollifield, eds. *Searching for the New France*. New York: Routeledge, 1992.

Ross, George, and Jane Jenson. "French Rainbows: Towards a New 'New Left' in France," *Socialist Review* 88.1 (1988): 98–104.

Ross, George, Stanley Hoffmann, and Sylvia Malzacher, eds. *The Mitterrand Experiment*. Cambridge: Polity Press, 1987.

———. *Workers and Communists in France*. Berkeley: University of California Press, 1982.

Rudig, Wolfgang, and P. D Lowe. "The Withered Greening of British Politics: A Study of the Ecology Party." *Political Studies* 34 (1986): 262–84.

Sainteny, Guillaume. "Chez les écologistes la désunion fait la force." *Revue politique et parlementaire* 958 (1992): 28–34.

———. *Les Verts*. Paris: Presses Universitaires de France, 1991.

———. "Les dirigeants écologistes et le champ politique." *Revue française de science politique* 37.1 (1987): 21–32.

Sale, Kirkpatrick. *The Green Revolution*. New York: Farrar, Strauss and Giroux, 1992.

Sartori, Giovanni. *Parties and Party Systems*. Cambridge, Mass.: Cambridge University Press, 1976.

Schama, Simon. *Landscape and Memory*. New York: Alfred A. Knopf, 1995.

Scharf, Thomas. *The German Greens: Challenging the Consensus*. Oxford: Berg, 1994.

Shull, Tad. "The Ecologists in the Regional Elections: Strategies Behind the Split." *French Politics and Society* 10.2 (1992): 13–29.

Smelser, Neil. *Theory of Collective Behavior*. New York: Free Press, 1962.

Tarrow, Sidney. *Struggle, Politics, and Reform*. Ithaca, N.Y.: Cornell Studies in International Affairs, 1989.

———. *Democracy and Disorder: Protest and Politics in Italy, 1965–1975*. Oxford: Clarendon, 1989.

———. "National Politics and Collective Action: Recent Theory and Research in Western Europe and the United States." *American Review of Sociology* 14 (1988): 421–40.

Tilly, Charles. *From Mobilization to Revolution*. Ann Arbor: University of Michigan Press, 1977.

Touraine, Alain. *The Voice and the Eye*. Trans. Alan Duff. New York: Cambridge University Press, 1982.

———. *Anti-nuclear Protest*. Trans. Peter Fawcett. Cambridge, Mass.: Cambridge University Press, 1980.

———. *The May Movement*. New York: Random House, 1971.

Veen, Hans-Joseph, and Jürgen Hoffmann. *Die Grünen zu Beginn der neunziger Jahre: Profil und Defizite einer fast etablierten Partei*. Bonn: Bouvier, 1992.

Les Verts. *Les Verts et l'économie*. Alain Lipietz, dir. of pub. Paris, 1992.

———. *Les Verts et les migrations: pour que les frontières tombent*. Maguitte Dinguirard, dir of pub. Paris, 1992.

———. *Les Verts et l'énergie*. Alain Fousseret, dir. of pub. Paris, 1990.

———. *Les Verts et l'Europe: pour une Europe des régions et des peuples solidaires*. Yves Cochet, dir. of pub. Paris, 1989.

———. *Les Verts et l'éducation*. Cochet, dir. of pub. Paris, 1989.

———. *Les Verts et la santé*. Cochet, dir. of pub. Paris, 1989.

———. *Les Verts et les transports*. Cochet, dir. of pub. Paris,1989.

———. *La choix de la vie*. Paris, 1989.

———. *Les Verts et la nature*. Guy Hascoët, dir. of publication. Paris, 1988.

———. *Les Verts et le tiers monde*. Hascoët, dir. of publication. Paris, 1988.

———. *Les Verts et l'agriculture*. Cochet, dir. of pub. Paris, 1988.

———. *Les Verts et la défense*. Cochet, dir. of pub. Paris, 1988.

Waechter, Antoine. Interview. *l'Heure de la verité*. France Antenne 2. 2 Feb., 1992.

———. *Dessine-moi une planête*. Paris: Albin Michel, 1990.

Weber, Max. *Economy and Society*. Ed. Gunther Roth and Hans Wittich. Berkeley: University of California Press, 1968.

———. *From Max Weber*. Trans. and ed. H. H. Gerth and C. Wright Mills. New York: Oxford University Press, 1946.

Whiteside, Kerry H. "The Resurgence of Ecological Thought in France." *French Politics and Society* 13.3 (1995): 43–58.

Wiesenthal, Helmut. *Realism in Green Politics*. Ed. John Ferris. Manchester, UK: Manchester University Press, 1993.

Wood, Ellen Meiksins. *The Retreat from Class: A New "True" Socialism*. London: Verso, 1986.

Wright, Erik Olin. *Class, Crisis and the State*. London: Verso, 1979.

Index